TOWARD A NEW UNDERST

AN UNFINISHED JOURNEY

BOOK 1

Through ADVENT *to* EPIPHANY

SERMONS BY TED BISHOP & JOHN CHURCHER

With Notes and Questions for Group Discussion

Edited by Betty Saunders

ISBN 978 1 4461 4398 8

Typeset in Stone Serif and Stone Sans
by Patricia Saunders, Huntingdon

Published and printed by
www.lulu.com

A Prayer for the Journey

Lord God, you have called your servants
to ventures of which we cannot see the ending,
by paths as yet untrodden,
through perils unknown.
Give us faith to go out with good courage,
not knowing where we go,
but only that your hand is leading us
and your love supporting us;
through Jesus Christ our Lord, Amen.

TABLE OF CONTENTS

A PREFACE

There were two factors that led to the production of this series of booklets:

> one was that the three of us were discovering how the latest New Testament studies and post-liberal theology coming mostly from the USA was enlightening our understanding of the Christian Gospel and (for the two of us who were regularly preaching) illuminating our preaching;

> the other was the discovery by Betty, the editor, following a letter by her in the *Methodist Recorder* in October 2008, that there is a real although hidden hunger among the Methodist people, and probably among people in other denominations, for access to this more radical theological teaching.

Through friendship with the two preachers she was aware of the serious study that went into each sermon which made the sermons worthy of wider circulation and, through the response to her letter in the *Methodist Recorder*, she was also aware of a serious lack of inexpensive group discussion material that takes into account post-liberal New Testament scholarship and theology.

The origin of these studies in sermon form had the advantage that they were composed, not for students in an academic setting who might be prepared to read large theological books, but for presentation to the random mixture of people in ordinary congregations. The theology in the sermons might be unfamiliar but was well digested by the preacher before presentation and always involved a suggested application to everyday life. The questions are intended to draw out ideas and information that may be new to the group and there are longer notes on some key issues that arise.

Although both preachers habitually follow the Lectionary they also frequently refer to parallel versions of the same story or theme in other Gospels or Old Testament readings. The sermons chosen follow the themes of the Christian year rather than the Lectionary readings for any one year but the parallels that make them relevant for other years are noted and easy to find. If anyone wishes to read current sermons by these preachers they are to be found on John Churcher's website, **PermissionToSpeak.org.uk**, and by request from Ted Bishop, **ted@tedbishop.co.uk**.

We have all three been engaged in a journey of faith and have found that, when we are not afraid to question previous assumptions and formulations composed by the Church for earlier generations, the result is not a negative loss of faith but an honest discovery of new depths of meaning and relevance for our day. We have therefore adopted as the prayer for our series the prayer that appears on the page following the title page. We use it with kind permission from the publishers of the *Lutheran Worship Book* from which we have taken it.

CHRIST THE KING 1

The Parable of the Sheep and the Goats

Introductory note

The first study is an exposition of a parable attributed to Jesus and unique to St Matthew's Gospel. It is set within the framework of the expectation of the Apocalyptic Last Judgement and End of the World that is the traditional subject for the Sunday before Advent. Scholars disagree about whether either the parable itself or its apocalyptic setting goes back to Jesus himself.

Beginning with Albert Schweitzer's famous book, *The Quest of the Historical Jesus*, many scholars in the last century thought that, although Jesus may not have spoken of his own Second Coming before his disciples knew of his Crucifixion and Resurrection, he did share the current Jewish expectation of the imminent arrival of the kingdom of God to be ushered in by the Messiah – a belief exemplified by the preaching of John the Baptist.

It would be the Shepherd King (the new David) who would come in glory to make the judgement. This was the Messiah described in the Matthew passage as the 'Son of Man' – referring back to Daniel 7.13. After their hopes were dashed by the Crucifixion and their hopes again raised by their conviction of his Resurrection this expectation was transferred to a Second Coming. Some more recent scholars think that the expectation was not shared by Jesus himself but originated in the Christian community after the Resurrection which in itself was regarded as a sign of the times, an expected 'End of Time' event. The traumatic experiences of the Jewish Revolt that culminated in the destruction of the Temple in 70 CE (about the time when Mark was writing the first of the Gospels) will have further encouraged these expectations.

Read
Matthew 25.31–46
Daniel 7.9–14 (A book of stories and prophecies set in the time of
Exile under the Babylonian emperor, Nebuchadnezzar, 605–562 BCE,
but written in the time of oppression under the Greek Seleucid ruler,
Antiochus IV, 175–164 BCE.)
1 Thessalonians 4.14–17 (Written about 50 CE.)

Sermon
This parable of the Sheep and the Goats is probably one of the best
known. May I ask how many of you remember this? Including
today? All of us, of course. Just remember *that* for a moment: we all
are familiar with this parable.

I can recall *vividly* the first time this parable really struck me. It
was about forty years ago – you see my long-term memory is very
good. We had returned from Burma and one of the responsibilities
all missionaries, as we were *then* called, had was to promote the
work of the Overseas Division of the Methodist Church and to
respond to requests to take Missionary Services, often a weekend,
during furlough. I returned on 1 April 1965. Now that's an inter-
esting date! There were five months available before I 'went into
circuit' in this country.

Looking though the advocacy material made available by MCOD
there was a film strip – remember those? They have returned via the
computer to view our photographs. There was one about Methodist
Church social work in Hong Kong entitled 'In as much …'

I knew the reference and I expect we can all complete the quota-
tion in one or other of its translations, and began to wonder about
its appropriateness. Some Bible translators take the Greek phrase
'these my brothers' to mean 'people in general', others believe it
refers to Jesus' own disciples. Let's leave aside for a moment the
recipients of their kindness and focus on the utter surprise of these
Good Samaritans at being commended for their kindnesses.

Over the intervening forty years I have thought about this parable from time to time and I came to think it very strange that it was

included in the Gospels at all, actually only in Matthew. However, I have often failed to get others to grasp the point I was making. Let me try it on you!

Once a Christian has heard this parable it doesn't apply to him/her! And by the same argument those it applies to will *never* hear it!

Does that make sense? *Someone explain.*

Put it another way: once a Christian has heard this parable s/he ought never to claim that kindnesses are done to someone because the recipient is Jesus incognito! Imagine yourself hungry, unclothed, in prison and so on and learning that you are a just an object of charity because the do-gooder somehow views you as Jesus in disguise!

One world-renowned person in line for sainthood constantly used this text; in fact it was virtually her motto.

So there's my problem.

More recently I wondered whether the parable was an answer to the oft-asked question: 'What happens to kind people who die without ever having heard of Jesus?' That's a question which implies a very narrow understanding of God by people who themselves would consign even the very good non-Christians to eternal fire!

In no way am I suggesting that such compassion described in the parable should *not* be the actions of followers of Jesus but that the motivation is not as I have described.

Of course we could stand this parable on its head and say that the Good-Samaritan-like sheep were actually good Christians who naturally did all these compassionate acts and who would never for a moment think them special in any way or who need a subterfuge, an incentive, to act in that way!

Now, having clarified one or two things, let's turn to a fresh look at this parable.

I think the first thing we notice is that this is set in *the End-Time*.

> When the Son of Man comes in his glory, and all the angels with
> him, then he will sit on the throne of his glory. All the nations
> will be gathered before him, and he will separate people one from

another as a shepherd separates the sheep from the goats, and he will put the sheep at his right hand and the goats at the left (verses 31–32).

Each of the Gospels has a section which reflects the End-Time, *but* some of the most memorable phrases are those used in Handel's *Messiah*, such as:

> I know that my Redeemer liveth and that He shall stand at the last day upon the earth … in my flesh I shall God [section 45] – Job 19.25–26.

> The trumpet shall sound and the dead shall be raised … [section 47] – Thessalonians 4.16.

> Blessing and honour and glory and power be unto him that sitteth upon the throne … [section 58] – Revelation 5.13.

All great stirring stuff and in two of them we recognise words from the Letters of Paul.

Such beliefs are summarised in the Nicene Creed: '… [Jesus] is seated at the right hand of the Father. He will come again in glory to judge the living and the dead, and his kingdom will have no end.'

Now this would be a whole series of *lectures* to cover this subject. We haven't the time and I guess you are not that interested, and *I* haven't the competence! But I recall the only heresy trial in recent Methodist history, perhaps even the last, was about fifty or sixty years ago and concerned the views of the Revd Francis Glasson on this subject, though what he said and wrote is probably acceptable today – or at least not heretical – but don't ask me what it was!

But what constantly interests people is the purpose of it all: 'Where are we going?' Ecology and climate change are the new 'frighteners' with their new message of 'repent of the way we are treating the earth or we shall all disappear in a great puff of smoke, or, at the best – or is it the worst? – a gradual degradation and slow death along with everything else.

The comparatively recent millennium change from the twentieth to the twenty-first century produced a host of predictions about The End. Extraordinary, to us, religious cults came into being to await the Last Day, climbing hills or mountains to be the first to see the rising sun of the very last day! Others couldn't wait and committed corporate suicide or were mass-murdered by their leaders. And so the list goes on, and the New Year of 2001 came and the world carried on.

What all these have in common, with all their strange-to-us ways, is a belief that history will not fizzle out but will come to a *purposeful* end; God's kingdom will dawn and the believers will reign with Christ. There are as many variations of this scenario as there are religious groups. And that's only the Christian ones. Add to it Jewish and Muslim believers.

To those of these Abrahamic faiths their history is one of real encounters with God and they look forward to further encounters until The End, the consummation of all things, takes place!

Jewish *Christians* shared this belief of promise, an event in history to which they could look *forward* with expectation and *share* through repentance and belief. Jesus Christ was the one who declared that the kingdom *would* come and invited, encouraged his followers to pray for it, an invitation that is encapsulated in the first sentence of the Lord's Prayer: 'Your kingdom come ...' though without any specifics.

It is not surprising then that when the Gospels came to be compiled after the catastrophic, apocalyptic destruction of Jerusalem and the Temple in the years 70–74 CE that End of Time pronouncements would be incorporated in them although they do not seem to be there in the pre-Gospel writings. An example of this is in The Gospel of Thomas and is referred to later. Mark first with 13.5–37, and then Matthew and Luke with Matthew 24.4–36 and Luke 17. 22–37 and 21.8–36, respectively in which they *imagined* what Jesus would have said to *them* in *their* situation of impending doom.

Before the compilation of the Gospels Paul had already begun to incorporate such a belief in his writings to the Young Churches, an expectation that is guaranteed through their experience of the Spirit of God (see 2 Corinthians 5.5, although some scholars dispute whether this is Pauline). I suppose in our financially orientated world we might call it a divine 'down payment'.

As the Christian communities became increasingly non-Jewish, composed of people with a background of Greek religion, and the years went by with no fulfilment of these views taken over from the Jewish believers, the belief in a kingdom of God to come was replaced by a kingdom of God that was already here.

One recent writer vividly describes the situation thus: the apocalyptic ideas took the role of inherited furniture, handed down to believers and not to be discarded, but no longer treasured (Lampe, quoted in 'Transforming Mission', p. 196, *Paradigm Shifts in Theology of Mission* by David J. Bosch). In fact these ideas were *so* treasured that they became part of the historic creeds and have caused endless problems to this day. Hence the current resurgence of 'you must believe everything that is written down' Christian communities and the endless controversies about what it all means and whether *it has any real meaning for today*.

That is finally and briefly what I would like to address.

The parable with which we began – that of the sheep and the goats – is set in the Last Days, and thus gives rise to many questions, not least whether Jesus was into the current Jewish belief system regarding final and impending dénouement. The argument on this between biblical scholars rolls on but there is a credible case for believing that Jesus made a different claim that is recorded in the earlier-than-Mark *Gospel of Thomas* (see pages 69–70).

In Logion 113 of the Gospel of Thomas we read:

> [Jesus'] disciples said to him, 'When will the [Father's] imperial rule come?' 'It will not come by watching for it. It will not be said "Look here!" or "Look there!" Rather the Father's imperial rule is spread out on the earth but people don't see it.'

Luke 17.20–21 makes the same point and, in another, 'If I by the finger of God cast out demons then the kingdom of God has come among you'.

Jesus constantly makes plain that his hearers need eyes to see and ears to hear. And *here* is another case in point. These are awkward sayings that provide a counterweight to the view that Jesus supported popular End Days beliefs.

Now to get back to sheep and the goats ... stripping off the apocalyptic casing we have a parable that contrasts those who live a life of compassion without making a song and dance about it with those who did nothing of the kind. It seems to me that we have here a typical Jesus story contrasting the life of the Pharisees with those whose caring nature springs out of the close life they live with others, that is the poor of the land, the dispossessed, the marginalised.

Compare this parable with the poor widow making her donation in the Temple poor box and the ostentatious man waving his large cheque around! Or with the man who is ashamed to lift up his eyes to God in prayer in the presence of a self-righteous Pharisee quoting his prayer book!

I mentioned hours ago, it seems, some other possible explanations of this parable but I think now we may have got to the heart of it, don't you? And doesn't that make sense today? And give *you* hope?

Questions for discussion

1   What do you think about the first point suggesting that the parable has encouraged an inappropriate motivation for Christian service?

2   To what extent do you think that this parable applies only to Christians?

3   What do you think is the main point of the parable and its relevance today?

CHRIST THE KING 2

The Book of Revelation

Read
Revelation 1.4–20
Revelation 17.4–6
Revelation 18.9–10, 21–24

Sermon
In this study we will look beyond the Lectionary reading and consider in general the final book in the Christian Testament, the Book of Revelation.

It used to be thought that the author was John the beloved disciple of Jesus, but most contemporary liberal Bible scholars doubt such authorship. Neither was the author the same man who had, at about the same time, written the Gospel of John and the three letters attributed to John – the content and styles of writing are very different. Most contemporary liberal Bible scholars now agree that the author of the Book of Revelation was a John who lived with his Christian community on the eastern Mediterranean island of Patmos, hence the authorship is now attributed to 'John of Patmos'.

The Book of Revelation is often thought of as an apocalypse – and as a prophecy of the End of Time. However, there were dozens of similar Jewish apocalypses written between 200 BCE and 100 CE – apocalyptic literature was two a penny over these three centuries. If the Book of Revelation was an apocalypse, John of Patmos was doing nothing new. But when we come to study books such as Revelation there are different ways in which they can be read – as literal truth or as metaphor; as future event or as comment on the signs of the times of the writing. The more conservative and fundamentalist

Christians of the Christian Right, often take the Book of Revelation as literal truth and as a prophecy of an event that is still to come. It is frightening to realise that the American Christian Right has often been over-represented in its influence upon the political situation in the most powerful nation on earth. It greatly influenced Ronald Regan when he was President of the USA and, even more worryingly, seemed to influence the policy decisions of the Bush administration. According to some commentators, the Christian Right did not have to lobby George W. Bush – he called on it before making momentous decisions and it was its influence that encouraged George W. to say that God had told him to invade Iraq.

But what has all this political rambling got to do with the Book of Revelation? Just the little matter of the Battle of Armageddon that is foretold in the Book of Revelation as a necessary precursor to the return of Jesus in glory. The Christian Right says that it will be on the Plain of Megiddo in Israel where there will be a major battle between good and evil. There will be an army of 200 million that will come from the east – from the Islamic countries who were seen to be part of George W. Bush's 'axis of evil' – and they were seen as the enemies of Christianity and had to be defeated by the might of 'Christian' America.

And defeated they will be, according to the Christian Right's interpretation of the Revelation prophecy. With all the power that can be unleashed in conventional and nuclear warfare, the President of the USA can destroy this earth dozens of times over and the attitude of many leaders of the Christian Right is that nuclear warfare is the obvious tool of God to defeat the eastern enemies. Many leaders of the Christian Right seem positively to encourage the nuclear holocaust of Armageddon because when it comes, Jesus will return and the righteous (that is, *sic* those who are Christian) will be snatched up into the heavens to meet Jesus in the sky. It is the eastern enemies who will perish in the nuclear nightmare. And this End-Time horror is mainly based upon two Bible verses. The first is 2 Peter 3.7: 'God has commanded the present heavens and earth to remain until the day of judgement. Then they will be set on fire, and ungodly people will be destroyed.' The second is Revelation 16.16: 'And he gathered them together into a place called in the Hebrew tongue Armageddon.' That is the danger of reading the Book of Revelation as a prophecy of things still to come. And such interpretation should be resisted at all costs. Blasphemy is the insulting or offending of God – and the Christian Right's literal interpretation of the Book of Revelation is a blasphemy as it abuses the nature of the One God of all people, the God that is Unconditional and Sacrificial Love revealed completely in Jesus.

I cannot interpret the Book of Revelation as a prophecy of things still to come. From my studies I am sure that it was a heavily coded book to encourage and to protect the followers of Jesus who were being persecuted by Rome and its succession of Emperors, and by the rulers of the Jewish synagogues who expelled Gentile and Jewish Christians from their places of worship. The Book of Revelation was a book written for its times – it was not written directly for us. However, as we struggle with the Spirit to interpret the ancient writing and to attempt to hear what the Spirit is saying to us in our days through the human words of John of Patmos, then these words can become sacred for us. According to many of our contemporary liberal scholars, such as John Dominic Crossan, Jesus and his followers were non-violent subversives in both the politics and religion of their time. It was his condemnation of the political and religious authorities that took Jesus to the Cross. According to many of our contemporary liberal Bible scholars, the battle for the early followers of Jesus was between accepting Jesus or Caesar as God, and living accordingly.

The early followers of Jesus lived on the edge of society, challenging the injustice of the political and economic domination systems. Jesus stood up for the underdogs – for the oppressed, for tax collectors and publicans, for sinners and lepers, for foreigners and women – Jesus brought those who were rejected by the political and religious establishments of his day right into the centre of his concern and claimed that God's kingdom belonged to such as these. At the time of Jesus, Rome dominated and exploited those whom it had defeated in war and conquest. The Roman Emperors believed that they ruled others because the gods had willed it to be so. Roman Emperors before and after the time of Jesus were self-proclaimed gods. Alexander the Great, some 300 years before Jesus, had been proclaimed Son of the Great God Zeus – another virgin birth perhaps? A decade or so before the birth of Jesus, Julius Caesar had been proclaimed God. After the death of Julius Caesar there was civil war within the Roman Empire and this was brought to an end by the victory of Augustus who ushered in the Pax Romana. As a result, in 9 BCE, probably five years before the birth of Jesus, Augustus was declared 'the most divine Caesar – the Saviour' – and the birthday of Augustus was declared to be the good news (the gospel) for the entire world. Does this ring any Christmas bells for you?

Jesus never claimed himself to be God. That was a title placed upon him after his death when his followers struggled to understand their experiences of the uniqueness of Jesus of Nazareth. And through their struggles to understand they arrived at the declaration that Jesus could only have been the Son of God and therefore they made him the Christ of the Church. The Book of Revelation is carefully coded and crafted to encourage the Christian readers that the exploiting and oppressive Roman Empire would not last forever because it was based upon the false gods of the Emperors. And there was only One true God, and only one ultimate victory, and that was to be found in the God experienced in Jesus.

As a codebook the number 7 is used often – 7 churches to whom the letters are written; 7 stars and 7 lamp stands; 7 trumpets; 7 seals that are broken open. There are 7 states of blessedness or happiness; 7 hymns of praise; 7 different types of people; 7 references to the altar, the place of sacrifice; 7 statements about the return – the Second Coming of Jesus. And in Revelation 12 we read of the archangel Michael battling and defeating the great dragon – now accepted by contemporary liberal scholars as a reference to the Roman Empire. And then in Revelation 13 a beast with 7 heads takes the place of the dragon. This beast comes out of the water and dominates the earth. And according to John of Patmos, the number of the beast is 666. And what is the significance of 666? Scholars tell us that the Hebrew alphabet was assigned numerical instead of phonetic value. This was called *gematria* and was used in Hebrew and Christian Testaments, and 500 years later in Islamic writings. And Bible scholars tend to agree that when decoded, 666 represented 'Caesar Nero' who had been persecuting Christians some thirty years after the first Easter.

There are other coded descriptions, for example 'Babylon the Great'. And what did the Babylonians do in 586 BCE? They destroyed Jerusalem and the Temple. And what did the Romans do in 70 CE? They destroyed Jerusalem and the Temple. When John of Patmos reminded his readers that from defeat the people of Yahweh God overcame the Babylonians and their domination system, John was encouraging his readers that the same would happen to Rome. Babylon was the coded name for the Roman Empire. And the literature, both ancient and modern at the time of John of Patmos, told mythical stories of the battles between good and evil, for example between the God Apollo and the Python; the literature told of seven-headed beasts and serpents and monsters rising from the sea. But they are not only in the mythical literature, they are there in the oldest Book of the Hebrew Scriptures, the Book of Psalms, 74.12–13. They are there in Isaiah 27.1 and 30.7 and 51.9. John of Patmos knew the ancient myths and the stories of the Hebrew scrolls and he was reinterpreting these and applying them to his vision of the times in which he was living.

John of Patmos said that there will be a new heaven and a new earth and a new Jerusalem, all ushered in by the return of the 'Lamb who was slain' (Isaiah 53.7) by the Romans on Calvary's Cross. The central message of John of Patmos in this Book of Revelation is that in the experiences of the political and economic domination system of Rome it appeared as though Caesar was God – but John was declaring, that despite the appearances to the contrary, Jesus was God. John was encouraging his persecuted readers that, one day, Jesus would come again and over throw the evil of Roman imperialism and all that went with its domination systems. And so, to his readers, John says 'hang in there – don't give up even if persecution takes you the way of the cross – for in Jesus there is the ultimate and eternal victory'. The Book of Revelation is unnecessarily spiritualised by Christian fundamentalists when it really is a book of encouragement to subversive action.

So how can we apply the teaching and the myths and the codes of the Book of Revelation to the way in which we live today? As followers of the way of Jesus, how can we confront systems of domination that stop people achieving the fullness of humanity that is their God-given right? It may mean challenging the IMF, the World Bank and the World Trade Organisation over decisions and commitments to free trade that are neither fair nor free for the poorest people on this planet. It means buying fairly traded products whenever possible. It may mean being accountable for my ecological footprint upon this earth. It means standing up for the underdog no matter who or where that person happens to be. It may mean joining the annual Amnesty International letter-writing campaign on behalf of prisoners of conscience, no matter who or where they are.

In all these ways, as we live God's kingdom no matter what the cost to ourselves, we shall be blessed.

The message of John of Patmos is not some pious prophecy of the End of Time events still to come. The message is simple – the inhuman domination systems represented by Rome and its Emperors will be defeated as each one of us takes our responsibility as followers of the way of Jesus to work and to pray for the end of political and economic exploitation – and to work for peace and justice for all people. That is the real challenge of the Book of Revelation – so let us live that challenge day by day, constantly countering the evil of the Christian Right's interpretation of the Book of Revelation. Amen.

Questions for discussion

1 To what extent are you persuaded by the interpretation of the Book of Revelation as primarily a coded message of encouragement for Christians suffering persecution under the Romans?

2 Should we look for 'Signs of the **End Time**' as many have done at critical points in history? If not, does it have any relevance for us today?

3 Do we think that there will be a 'Last Judgement' when the good will be vindicated and rewarded and the evil will be punished and finally vanquished?

4 To what extent is the 'kingdom of God' to be found here and now? Has God made us responsible for bringing it in, each in our own generation, as the study suggests?

STUDY THREE

ADVENT SUNDAY

The Coming Kingdom

The visions of the prophets known as Isaiah

Read

Isaiah 2.1–5

Light a candle

Jesus is the light of the world who comes into the darkness of our lives bringing newness of life, and offering us all sure ground for hope. This candle reminds us that we are called to be a light to the world as we reflect to others the light of the Perfect Love that is God shown fully in Jesus.

Sermon

The first candle of Advent is traditionally the candle of Expectation and Hope. In Methodism we often think of the first Sunday in Advent as the day to remember Abraham and the Patriarchs – the Fathers of the Jewish religion – the root that later gave birth to both Christianity and Islam. Today's candle burns as the symbol of the expectation of the coming of the Messiah that winds its way throughout the Hebrew Scriptures that we call the Old Testament. But we also remember that within the teachings of Christianity that same Messiah has come already in Jesus of Nazareth. The candle is also the symbol that darkness can never destroy the light, and it represents the Hope that Messiah will one day bring peace and justice to this broken and incomplete world. But the Lectionary readings from the Book of Isaiah offer us a glimpse into the ancient theme of Expectation and Hope for a nation that regularly experienced the trauma of defeat and foreign occupation.

The Book of Isaiah is presented in our Bibles as one book but contemporary Bible scholarship suggests that there were two, perhaps even three or more authors. First Isaiah wrote what we have as chapters 1 through to 39 in the eighth century before Jesus. Isaiah 6.1 says that Isaiah was called in the year 742 BCE, in the year in which King Uzziah died. First Isaiah lived and prophesied in Jerusalem and his whole life was overshadowed by the growing might of the Assyrian Empire. Indeed, 21 years after First Isaiah was called to prophesy, the Assyrian Empire defeated the tribe of Israel. This left Judah as the one surviving tribe of Yahweh's people.

The reasons given for the two-author interpretation of our single Book of Isaiah include the changes in both the style and in the historical context of writing between chapters 39 and 40. Second Isaiah appears to be writing during the aftermath of another defeat of Judah, this time at the hands of the Babylonians that resulted in the deportation and exile of the people. And this exile occurred from 586 BCE.

Second or Deutero-Isaiah begins at chapter 40 and is written to the Judah exiles living in Babylon. The earlier prophecies concerning the destruction of the Jerusalem Temple have been fulfilled. This dates Second Isaiah between 597 and 538 BCE. No wonder Second Isaiah is writing to comfort the defeated and exiled people.

Those scholars who claim that there was a third author suggest that Second Isaiah finished writing at chapter 55 and Third or Trito Isaiah contributed chapters 56 to 66.

To complicate things further, the general agreement is that Trito-Isaiah was actually several unknown authors writing between 525 and 475 BCE. It is even thought by some scholars, that some of the material of Trito-Isaiah came from a much later time, during 375 to 250 BCE, when Judah had become Palestine and was under Greek rule until replaced by Egyptian rule in 301 BCE.

The scholars who argue for a third Isaiah do so on the basis that the emphasis of the earlier chapters was upon Yahweh God, the God of the Jews, who excluded all those who were not Jews – but from chapter 55 to the end of the book the emphasis changed to include these Gentiles as well as Jews as being children of the same God.

We cannot properly understand the Hebrew or Christian Testaments unless we know that of the 66 books and letters that comprise our Bible, some 53 of them (that's 80 per cent) were written while the writers were living as defeated people under the oppression of foreign powers. This means that our Scriptures are primarily the thoughts and experiences of people who were defeated and oppressed. They remembered their past, lamented their present and anticipated a glorious future when they would be free at last. To forget this is to misunderstand and misinterpret our Bible and its relevance for us and for this broken and incomplete world today.

But having quoted the scholarship, notice that today's Lectionary reading by First Isaiah seems to go against the scholarship of Second and Third Isaiah! Here First Isaiah speaks concerning the end of earthly time. But First Isaiah could only write from within the science and history and language of his times, and it is quite obvious that he knew nothing of the potentially disastrous consequences of global warming, but in his vision, First Isaiah expected that there will come a time when people will flock to Jerusalem saying, 'Come, let us go up to the mountain of the Lord, to the house of the God of Jacob. He will teach us his ways, so that we may walk in his paths.'

Isaiah says that God's Law, as interpreted by the descendants of Jacob, will go to all people starting from Jerusalem. And when this happens God will be the judge between the nations and will settle disputes between people. This will be a pilgrimage towards peace.

When this sermon was preached we had just seen the faltering first steps of yet another attempt on this pilgrimage towards peace when Palestinian and Israeli leaders met for talks in the USA. And yet the key to success will not be based upon George W. Bush's attempts to persuade the delegates to compromise. Peace does not rest upon who compromises the most – because compromise seldom settles long-standing problems for very long.

The success of this latest pilgrimage of peace must start with Third Isaiah's vision that there is One God of All in which all people accept that they are sisters and brothers of one another – Christian,

Jew, Muslim, Sikh, Hindu, Baha'i, Buddhist – and how can such sisters and brothers be at war with each other? And how can we, the rich sisters and brothers, sleep comfortably tonight knowing that others of our sisters and brothers are dying as a result of our political and economic systems that exploit the poor, causing hunger and exacerbating disease? Only when we all recognise the sisterhood and the brotherhood of all people will the central message of the Lectionary reading set for this first Sunday in Advent this year, have a chance of being fulfilled – only then will they 'beat their swords into ploughshares and their spears into pruning hooks'. Only then will nation 'not take up sword against nation, nor will they train for war any more' (Isaiah 2.4 NIV).

And when that day comes restless hearts will find rest; our anxious hearts will no longer be overcome; our incompleteness as humankind will find wholeness; those who have no hope will find their dreams fulfilled; those who are wounded will find healing; those who are broken-hearted will be comforted; those who are oppressed will finally be free. And peace and good will to all people will be the universal experience. What a vision for the future!

But let's be honest about this. Our Christian faith is rooted in both hope for the future and in the reality of here and now. And that Utopian vision of the future probably will be unrealised within our life times. But that vision is our responsibility to live today as followers of the way of Jesus. Just because we are unlikely to attain it is no reason for us not to try to attain it. We owe it to all our children and grandchildren; to all the generations that follow, that we play our part by living kingdom ways here and now. And it is as we live the Kingdom of Perfect Love and of justice and of peace, that all Isaiah's visions can be our daily experiences, no matter what befalls us.

It is as we daily live the Kingdom of Perfect Love, following the example of Jesus by walking in his footsteps, that our anxious, restless and troubled hearts and minds will find rest and peace in the ever presence of God; our incompleteness and imperfections will be replaced by the wholeness that is God; those who feel that they are losing hope will know that their dreams can be fulfilled in God; those who feel wounded or broken-hearted by the twists and turns of life will find comfort, healing and peace in God; and those who feel oppressed will be free in God.

Now none of this is empty 'pie in the sky one day when you die' theology – it is ours now as we live the way of Jesus – and as we live as kingdom people. This is the Advent Hope; it is not a hollow dream for some time in the future; it is the incarnational way of life; the way of life of God dwelling within each of us; the way of life that results from each one of us being Temples of the Spirit that is God. It is the incarnational way of life to be lived here and now.

The Christian faith is not about believing the unbelievable written in the times when people thought God was a superhuman being – the Great Old Man who sat just above the skies, written at a time when people thought that the world was flat and Hell was just beneath our feet. The Christian life is less about believing the unbelievable and more, much more, about living and working in the dirt and grime of every day life, getting our hands dirty to help others into the experience of the abundant life that is ours in Jesus. The Christian faith is not 'airy fairy' because it is grounded in the realities of life. Will you continue to work in the joy of the struggle to bring life today to all people everywhere?

Questions for discussion

1 Share with one another what your hopes are for the future – personally, as a church, for the world.

2 How realistic does the vision of Isaiah in this passage seem to you? What do you think we can do to help realise that vision?

STUDY FOUR

ADVENT 2

The Meaning of Advent

Read
Isaiah 40.1–11
Mark 1.1–8

Sermon

The Second Sunday of Advent is a time for looking forward to the celebration of the birth of Jesus, and also to what some Christians call the return or the Second Coming of Jesus. But we must remember that Advent is not something created by Jesus – it is the creation of the Church in the fourth century as part of the preparation for adult baptism.

But as we continue through another Advent Season we have to admit that something is seriously wrong with the Christian Church in this country. We have lost some 70 per cent of our regular worshippers over these past fifty years. Only 2 per cent of the population will be in church Sunday by Sunday. Only 6 per cent will attend church at least one Sunday a month. People have rejected the Church and the creeds and doctrines and teachings of the Church. We cannot go on preaching the same things and expecting to get a different result – a new revival.

Although many progressive Christians today genuinely love the Bible, there are at least two major challenges for the institutional Church today in regard to what we refer to as our Holy Book.

The first is that Christians too often interpret, or are expected to interpret, the Hebrew and Christian Testaments as factual truth. What Christians tend to avoid or simply have never been told is that both the Hebrew and Christian Testaments are made up of Midrash, that Jewish rabbinic literary device that took ancient stories from the Hebrew Testament and rewrote them and applied them to contemporary situations to help the listeners and readers better understand their situations; of myth, metaphor and poetry; of politics and economics; of history remembered and history interpreted; of many stories through which they try to explain the inexplicable about what they saw as their Yahweh God, the One beyond, coming to be with human beings. We need to understand that the Scriptures were not written to be interpreted as historical truth.

The second major challenge is that too few Christians take the Hebrew and Christian Testaments really seriously or study the Scriptures within the contexts of their writing. Congregations are often too content listening to the wisdom of their preachers rather than personally getting to grips with the written texts of our Hebrew and Christian Testaments. This often means that the Scriptures are ignored on a day-to-day living basis, or they are misapplied by pulling odd verses out of context and making them fit into a personal or corporate interpretation and experience of the contemporary world. But it is not always the fault of the congregations. The Church down the ages has created and maintained a dependency culture in which congregations depend upon their ministers and preachers to tell them about belief.

Another related problem is that, too often, preachers deny congregations access to contemporary biblical scholarship, perhaps because preachers reject it or are unaware of it, or fear for their future careers, or fear upsetting the listeners. And sadly, it is not unknown for some preachers to treat small or elderly congregations in a patronising manner, summed up in the words of a senior preacher who recently said to me, 'I believe what you say but this is not the place to say it – you will upset the elderly who have such a simple faith.' Nonsense – some of the most progressive-thinking people that I have come across over recent years are those in the third and fourth ages with time to think deeply about their spirituality whilst aging.

We turn now to the Lectionary readings set for today. In our last Study we looked at the composition of the Book of Isaiah in two or possibly three different historical contexts. They and our New Testament reading from Mark all tell us something about ourselves and also about the great love, mercy and grace from the One that Christians call 'God' and whom we meet fully in Jesus. But to understand these readings we need to have some more background information this time about the background to the New Testament reading.

Scholarly understanding of the order of the writing of the Christian Testament is that Paul's letters were written and Paul was executed before any of the Gospels in our New Testament were actually written. Mark's Gospel probably was the first of our four Gospels to be written. It is generally thought to have been written from within the Christian community based in Rome in the mid-60s immediately after the death of Peter and just before the great destruction of the Jerusalem Temple in 70 CE.

But other Bible scholars suggest that Mark was writing in the immediate aftermath of the destruction of the Jerusalem Temple. If the Gospel of Mark was written as late as 74 or 75, the writer was looking back with hindsight and was thus able to write into the mouth of Jesus 'the signs of the times' and the forewarnings of persecution some forty years before the actual events took place.

And there are other contemporary scholars who suggest that this passage is also a Second Advent passage, talking of the events at the climax of history: of the events that will happen at the end of the world as we know it. For these scholars and preachers who take this line, the important issue is that we do not inquire of God when this day will come, for that day and that hour is not made known to any human.

However, no matter how we understand the timing of the writing of Mark's Gospel, and whether or not this passage has anything to do with the End of Time, our responsibility as followers of the way of Jesus is to watch and to live the values of the kingdom of God in the here and now.

A Methodist minister once displayed a small 'tongue in cheek' poster in his office that said, 'Look busy – Jesus is coming'. Tongue in cheek it may have been, and whether or not we believe in the physical return of Jesus at the End of Time, the poster summed up an important truth – like the watchman on guard, we ought to be always on our watch, living daily in the expectation of the completion of the kingdom when we will all be like Jesus: lives full of compassion towards others; lives full of service and sacrifice offered to others; lives full of unconditional love and respect for others.

Also, as part of taking the Scriptures seriously, we need to approach our readings acknowledging a number of important issues.

First, we need to remember that Mark, Jesus and Isaiah, were Jews, brought up within the religion and culture of Judaism lived through times of persecution from foreign powers. It is important also to recognise that both our Old and New Testaments were primarily written by Jews for Jews within a context where things did not have to be historically true for them to be experienced as truth because they were interested in the meaning of the story rather than its factuality. The problem came when the early Churches ceased to be predominantly Jewish and their way of interpretation was no longer understood. The early Gentile Fathers of the Church often used allegory in their interpretation but their cultural background was Greek and the early development of Christian doctrine reflects Greek philosophical thought and mythology.

The second important point is that we have to face another question: was Isaiah in our chapter 40 reading prophesying concerning John the Baptist as the one who would speak 'in the wilderness, prepare the way for the LORD; make straight in the desert a highway for our God'? Or is this Mark, with the gift of hindsight looking back at this Isaiah passage and applying Midrash to John the Baptist? After all, verse 6 of our Isaiah reading today has a voice telling Second Isaiah to 'Cry out!' And Isaiah said, 'What shall I cry?'

I am convinced that this passage refers to Second Isaiah who, during the Babylonian Exile is offering hope to the hopeless; offering good news to Zion, to Jerusalem, and to the towns of Judah, saying, 'Here is your God who comes with power, and his arm rules for him. You will be free!' This is an example of how the Jews saw

Yahweh God as a carrot-and-stick God: when things were going well for the people then Yahweh God was pleased with them and blessed them with peace and success. However, when the people forgot the ways of Yahweh God, then the prophets saw their God as being jealous and captivity and destruction were heaped upon the people to bring them back to the ways of Yahweh.

Is this any real surprise that when the Jews saw Yahweh God as the carrot-and-stick God, both the Hebrew and Christian Testaments reflect the tradition in which they are confessing and regretting their sins and recognising that they themselves were unworthy of God's mercy? They understood that their sin was offensive to what they thought was their Yahweh God. They understood that this, their God, hated their sin. They believed that when they were cut off from their Holy God they needed God's mercy and grace or there was no way that they could come into Yahweh God's presence. They often thought that their good deeds in loving others still fell short of what they considered their Yahweh God called them to do. This is all alien and foreign to the majority of people living in the western world today. If we are to offer a relevant God to people today, I wonder how long can we continue proclaiming a carrot-and-stick God such as this?

But there is another way to interpret the Scriptures that may make them more relevant to our post-modern world today. Our sin is not the result of some original perfect creation in which Adam and Eve fell – this is in conflict with both our scientific advances and common sense. Our sin is the result of us being not yet fully human. We are still evolving to become the people who will live fully the kingdom ways of compassion, service, sacrifice and unconditional acceptance of others. The Gospel truth is that we can become more like Jesus of Nazareth, the One in whom his disciples experienced the fullness of humanity. This was so far beyond anything in their own lives that they concluded that Jesus was both human and God. It was in the fullness of humanity in Jesus that his followers experienced the Sacred. And that was the experience 2000 years ago and it is the truth that can be the experience for us today.

The truth of the Season of Advent for me is not so much in anticipating yet another celebration of the birth of Jesus, although this is important. Nor is it in anticipating some return of Jesus some-time in the future, as many progressive Christians doubt that there ever will be such a time. The truth of the Advent Season is that in the coming of Jesus 2000 years ago we have met the Sacred in a unique way. Our Advent calling is our daily calling, to live the Jesus Way of compassion, faith, generosity, hope, respect, service, sacrifice and unconditional love; it is for us to continue to live these values of the kingdom, because this is the great Advent message for all human-kind. Followers of Jesus today need to be open and prepared to think afresh about the creeds and doctrines of the Church. And as we do so, may we be blessed as we are Advent blessings to others.

Questions for discussion

1   If this is the first time you have come across the term 'Midrash', pause to read the explanatory note on page 26. Do you think that this may illuminate your understanding of the Gospels? Or is it so strange to our modern way of thinking that it will take a while to grasp how it was used? You will come across the idea many times in this series.

2   To what extent do you find it helpful or upsetting to under-stand the historical context of familiar New Testament stories and to know the order in which the books of the New Testament were written?

3   How different might your understanding of Jesus be if you were to read afresh the Christian Testament in the order in which it was written rather than the order in which it is printed?

4   What do you think about the preacher's statement that our sin is not the result of the 'Fall' of Adam and Eve but is a stage of evolution towards a true humanity?

Explanatory note on Midrash

'Midrash' is a Hebrew word meaning 'interpretation of the Torah' – the Torah being the Hebrew name for the first five books of the Old Testament. In the Greek version of the Old Testament that was in use in New Testament times, the word, 'Torah' is translated as the 'Law' but it is better understood as 'Instruction' or 'Teaching', intended for the guidance of 'God's people', the Jewish community.

Midrash already developed by rabbinic Judaism through rabbinic argument, debate and dialogue was adopted by Jewish Christians in the first century CE, (following the destruction of the Temple in 70 CE) and was and remains a very creative thought form. It became a literary genre in its own right and was the way in which ancient stories were explored and explained. Even in the time of Jesus, and for those Jews who followed him and were responsible for writing the Epistles and Gospels, it was already a major way in which ancient stories were interrogated and applied to life.

Midrash can be divided into two basic types, the first known as 'halakhah,' meaning 'to walk'. This was the rabbinic interpretation and assistance on how to walk the way that God required by the laws given by God and recorded in the Torah. The second form of Midrash is known as 'haggadah' which means 'to tell a story'.

But, whereas in the West we tend to state a principle or idea and then look for a story or picture to illustrate it, the Jewish writers in New Testament times might begin with the illustration and draw out its significance through conversation and debate.

'Story' is of crucial importance in every ancient culture and when people wrote about the past they were concerned not with historical accuracy as we understand it but with the meaning of the events they were relating.

It was only after the Enlightenment, beginning in the West in the seventeenth century CE, that history became a form of science, requiring evidence from verifiable early documents and archeological remains, and 'factuality' rather than 'meaning' became all-important. It was from this point onwards that Christian scholars began to be divided between the 'conservatives' who defended the historicity of the Gospels and the 'liberals' who looked for alternative explanations, some of them rather far-fetched and unconvincing. The Jewish context remained unexplored and hidden behind anti-Jewish prejudice until after the Second World War and the work of organisations like the Council of Christians and Jews (founded in 1942). This was followed by the work of scholars such as E. P. Sanders and Geza Vermes who began to interpret the Gospels in their Jewish context. The relevance of Midrash was noticed by a British scholar, Michael Goulder who shared his ideas with a Bishop of the American Episcopal Church, Jack Spong through whose books this understanding has become more widely known. Other scholars, and notably the scholars of the Centre for Christian and Jewish Relations based at Wesley House in Cambridge, have further enlarged our understanding.

An understanding of the place of 'story' in ancient cultures has been very fully explored by Karen Armstrong in her books on the history of religion and is most briefly presented in her *Short History of Myth* that is a concise gem of historical scholarship.

The Enlightenment has not destroyed humanity's love and need for 'story' to explain the meaning of life, although we now tend to make a strict dividing line between fact and fiction. The power and popularity of *The Lord of the Rings*, the Harry Potter books and Philip Pullman's *Dark Materials* are examples that come to mind and the division between fact and fiction has not prevented the development of tourist trails around the supposed historic sites of events in Dan Brown's *Da Vinci Code*!

His scientific mind-set did not prevent Darwin from reinterpreting the ancient symbol of the 'Tree of Life' that is found in most ancient religions and giving it a new meaning for our time.

The authors and editor are grateful to Lucy Hidveghyova for her research into Midrash that has greatly contributed to our thinking.

Truth and Unity

Read
Matthew 11.2–11
Acts 18.24—19.7

Sermon

I once heard it expressed that the post-Reformation Baptist Churches were founded by John the Baptist; a very strange appeal to antiquity that may have provided the speaker with a sense of pride!

What is not so strange is that until the beginning of the current Iraq war there were some 60,000 people in that country living south of Bagdad who honoured John the Baptist *above* Jesus and practised frequent baptism, by immersion of course. Known as Mandaeans they have almost been eliminated during the present conflict.

This year the BBC have carried a number of news items about the Mandaeans and on 5 November showed a picture of a baptism in the River Tigris by one of their priests. (For those who like to look these things up on the internet there are 500 pages of references!)

I may also have *other* news for you … there was a John the Baptist movement in what we sometimes call 'New Testament times'. We have read of some disciples of John the Baptist being assimilated into the emerging Christian community in Acts 18.24—19.7 (see above).

Apparently other groups continued to be loyal to John the Baptist and in some way competed with the Jewish-Christian communities. This is evident from the four Gospels which were compiled over a period of about 100 years or more from the time of Jesus. Mark, Matthew, Luke and finally John reveal increasing pressure to promote Jesus at the expense of John the Baptist; Luke's Gospel in particular, but John's Gospel too.

A simple comparison is between Jesus' call of the first disciples, Simon Peter and Andrew, in Mark's Gospel (1.16) and in John's Gospel written more than 100 years later (John 1.35–42) where we read that John the Baptist is said to have encouraged Andrew and one other unnamed disciple of his to follow Jesus.

We are familiar with the way the followers of a particular person seek to promote *their* leaders at the expense of another group with *their* leader. The supporters are sometimes doing this as a way to seek their *own* advantage, looking, perhaps in the case of politicians, for a place in the Cabinet of a future administration.

We see James and John doing the same thing, advancing their own careers, seeking a place on either side of Jesus when *his* kingdom comes! (Mark 10.35–40, Matthew 20.20–23, Luke 12.50.)

So let us turn to the Gospel reading and immediately the *final* verse will strike us as most unusual, so let's start *there*. It reads: 'Truly I tell you, among those born of women no one has arisen greater than John the Baptist; yet the least in the kingdom of heaven is greater than he.'

One commentator writes that 'Jesus is probably the only speaker in Christendom who would have called John the Baptist the greatest among all human beings' (*The Five Gospels – What did Jesus really say?*, p. 179) yet (my words now) the second part of the sentence ranking the Baptist less than the least in God's kingdom is probably one of the great put-downs of history!

So we can see straightaway the workings of the early Church leaders, in particular of those who compiled the Gospels. Spin is not a recent invention!

This passage is included here after the disciples have been sent on their mission (Chapter 10) and gives an opportunity to include this anecdote about John's enquiry and provides a useful introduction to Jesus' activities. The contrast between the two, John and Jesus, would have already been noted by Jesus' followers and John's too. Jesus wouldn't compare very favourably as far as the Jews were concerned! John appears to be more like the sort of prophetic figure they had been led to expect, a new Elijah perhaps!

Jesus on the whole is not portrayed as a 'look what a great fellow I am' sort of person, although in Luke's Gospel Jesus *is* described in the Nazareth synagogue incident as referring to a Scripture passage from Isaiah 61.2 as a sort of manifesto (Luke 4.16–30).

Here in Matthew we find a list of four quotations from different parts of the scroll of Isaiah that say the same thing (Isaiah 35.5–6, 29.18–19, 26.19 and 61.1).

There is some evidence, some say much evidence, that Matthew's Gospel came into being as sort of 'second lesson' for Jewish-Christians in Jerusalem and Judaea who continued to worship as a Jewish community would and as such followed the Jewish Religious Year passages that would depict and sustain the ministry of Jesus though not necessarily understood in a literal way to Jews and a way of putting scriptural 'flesh' on the bare bones of Jesus' life story, teaching, parables etc. The same claim is also made for the compilation of Luke's Gospel, but in this case the recipients would have been Jewish-Christians living in the Greek way among the cities of the Roman Empire together with Greek adherents [Hellenists] drawn to the Jewish and now Christian Way.

So the passage continues: This may not be what you were expecting of The Anointed One but it does make sense *so* 'blessed is [congratulations to] anyone who takes no offence at me' (verse 6). There are other times when Jesus is reported as defending this message of TLC, tender loving care, in a climate in which John's more robust message was likely to receive a more welcome response.

And then as the disciples of John leave the scene there is a sudden reversal in the argument. Now it is John's life style that receives approval. If you've been mistaken about Jesus it is just as likely that you have been mistaken about John the Baptiser as well! 'What did you go out into the wilderness to look at? A reed shaken by the wind? What then did you go out to see? Someone dressed in soft robes? Look, those who wear soft robes are in royal palaces. What then did you go out to see? A prophet? Yes, I tell you, and more than a prophet. This is the one about whom it is written, "See, I am sending my messenger ahead of you, who will prepare your way before you."'

We can't really see Jesus defending himself in quite the way the earlier statement to John's disciples describes it but this passage sounds exactly like Jesus defending someone *else*!

Then comes the sentence with which we began.

> Truly I tell you, among those born of women no one has arisen greater than John the Baptist; yet the least in the kingdom of heaven is greater than he.

So what is the kingdom of heaven referred to here? Does it mean the same as the 'kingdom of God'?

Does it refer to an earthly or heavenly, that is an *other worldly* realm? The picture language used a century or so later in the Revelation of St John has become, for some the *literal* description of a divine kingdom, both on earth and heaven – whatever that can refer to today when a three-decker universe: earth, heaven *above* and hell *below* is no longer the scientific way of viewing the universe.

What sort of demarcation is intended by this text 'yet the least in the kingdom of heaven is greater than John the Baptist?'

Given the survival through the first Christian century and beyond of a John the Baptist movement that I have referred to, it seems very likely that this sentence was introduced as a way to counter *their* influence and to enhance the community of the 'Followers of the Way' of Jesus in the second half of the first century and beyond.

We need, however, to draw some conclusions for *ourselves* from this passage that does not divide us from others, set *our* group of people apart as superior to others, nor create a sense of marginal - isation in those who feel they are being discriminated against for one reason or another.

We may feel we can find little in *our* experience or in the story of the Churches that will help us here, and certainly almost nothing in the history of the relationships between world faiths to guide us.

We may well think that this is uncharted territory!

However during the formative period of the very first communities of the Followers of the Way when the Gospels were beginning to take shape we have the Letters written by Paul which describe the tensions which existed between the emerging groups. The Acts of the Apostles purport to cover the same period but, written in retrospect, some of the rough corners have been rubbed off and there are passages which are inconsistent with Paul's Letters.

We have already looked briefly at Paul's description of his meeting with Apollos and other disciples of John the Baptist. It seems that they were easily convinced!

Others were obviously less persuadable seeing that John the Baptist's group continued.

A more tenacious group were the Jewish Christians in Jerusalem led by James the brother of Jesus. They were less willing to give up the Jewish dietary practices and circumcision or to mix readily with Gentile Christians. Paul was taken to task by them for his *relaxed* view and his confrontation with Peter who, it seems, ran with both the hares and hounds and is described *thus* in the Letter to the Galatians [Galatians 2.11–14].

Paul, it seemed was prepared to allowed them some degree of accommodation provided they did not try to try to insist on conformity. Reports of this attempt vary between the Letters and The Acts.

Another challenge to Paul's leadership, we must see it in this way, was that of ecstatic utterance. The existence of what is nowadays often called just 'tongues' or 'speaking in tongues' is a verifiable occurrence. It is mostly associated with charismatic churches, and described as a gift of the Spirit.

In Paul's day, and remember this was between the death of Jesus and the compiling of the Gospels, there were Christians for whom this gift was *the* Gift of the Spirit.

To *their* existence we owe chapters 12, 13 and 14 of Paul's Letter to the Corinthians, our *first* letter but almost certainly his *second*! Paul admits to such ecstatic utterance when he tries to get people to see that this was but one of the gifts of the Spirit, and part of the building blocks of the emerging Christian Community, not its destroyer. (See 1 Corinthians 14.13–19, especially verse 18!)

I guess that in some way the group of Disciples of John the Baptist were the first of the Christian Cults, if that means the allegiance of believers to a person as a cult figure and were able to believe that he – and it is always a 'he' – had *the* truth, the *whole* truth and *final* word. And this group was certainly not the last!

One of the marks of such cults is the *un*-churching of *all* other Christians.

And when even the largest and strongest Church declares others heretics then it too is *sectarian*!

When Paul, or most probably one of his closest colleagues, wrote in the Ephesians Epistle, 'Hold fast with the bonds of peace the unity that the spirit gives' [Ephesians 4.1–6] he was trying to hold together this diverse group of believers in an essential unity. Let the diversity be recognised and accepted as within the Church, part of the whole, the Body of Christ.

If the Ephesians Letter was written later than the indisputable Pauline letters and represents an attempt to maintain or retain the unity of the Christian communities this would tie in with the view of some scholars that Matthew's Gospel was also an attempt to both reflect the variety of views that were emerging in those communities, as Paul does, and to provide a reconciling document among the conservative, radical and isolationist Christian groups. These attempts to hold diversity in unity failed miserably.

Each fresh breakaway from that unity, the Body of Christ, was made because the group concerned had suddenly discovered '*the* truth, the whole truth and nothing but the truth!' And, it seems, each new breakaway from the essential Body of Christ did so because they had discovered *that* truth in the Bible! A process that has been going on for getting on for 2,000 years!

In every attempt to 'hold fast with the bonds of peace the unity that the Spirit gives', those who are 'accommodating', some would say willing to compromise, face a form of 'blackmail' from the rigorists.

The current example of this is the tension in the world-wide Anglican community.

Truth is being sacrificed, so it seems, to a specious form of unity.

Perhaps the time has come *regrettably* to abandon the pursuit of unity to pursue truth wherever it leads, trusting that although conclusions may sometimes be only proximate at least they are honest.

Perhaps Christmas is a very good time to start pursuing truth and discovering meaning!

Questions for discussion

1 Read the following Note on the place of the Gospels in synagogue worship when the early Christian Church was meeting in the synagogues.
Share your first reaction to this explanation.

2 Many of the ideas in these studies may be new to you and some writers and preachers who express these ideas are accused of stirring up dissension in the Church. How do we reconcile the pursuit of truth with the desire for unity?

3 There is a long-held Jewish tradition that 'Where two or three study the Torah (the Jewish Scriptures) together the Shekinah (the presence of God) is in their midst'. There is an expectation that there will be more than one valid interpretation and that truth arises from discussion of differing views.
Is this the way forward in the dilemma posed by this study?

Note on the theory that the Gospels were shaped by their use in synagogue worship in the early Jewish Church

In the fifth-century manuscript of Mark's Gospel, entitled the *Codex Alexandrinus* the text is broken up into 49 sections, each one numbered and titled. Michael Goulder and Jack Spong have studied this manuscript carefully and have concluded that it is a succession of Sabbath readings linked directly to the Jewish liturgical lectionary cycle.

To Goulder and Spong, the subject matter of Mark's Gospel was not a random selection of events remembered from the life of Jesus, nor was it a narrative myth but they were decided upon by the worship needs of the early Jewish Christian communities as they met in the Jewish synagogues along side those Jews who rejected the Messianic claims assigned to Jesus by early Jewish Christian leaders.

For example, Goulder and Spong suggest that by placing Mark 16, the Passion story of Jesus, to be read on what we call Easter Sunday, the rest of the *Codex Alexandrinus* sections fit into 49 weeks of the Jewish liturgy. Although reading Mark's Gospel as a Jewish Christian liturgy leaves approximately one third of the Jewish Sabbath cycle without comparable content, it is possible to identify which part of Mark applies to which part of the Jewish cycle.

A further example is that in the Jewish liturgical cycle, the book of Deuteronomy was read over twelve Sabbaths. Careful comparison between Deuteronomy and Mark 10—12 (the journey of Jesus and his disciples from Galilee to Jerusalem) demonstrates a mirror image or, perhaps, even Midrash at work. Examples include teaching on humility; schism within the fellowship; rules governing marriage and divorce; nurturing of children; affluence and possessions. Then in Mark 13 Jesus speaks of the imminent arrival of the Messiah and the end times of this world. This would have been the Jewish Christian reading for the exact Jewish Sabbath dealing with the time when the old gave way to the new.

When considering why the later Gospel of Matthew is longer than Mark's, Spong suggests that additional stories were included to complete the gaps between Mark and the Jewish lectionary Sabbath cycle. It should be noted that most of the additional material in Matthew's Gospel (and then copied by Luke) comes either side of Mark's account: the genealogy and the birth stories of Jesus, and the period post-Easter to Pentecost. The *Codex Alexandrinus* edition of Matthew's Gospel contains 69 named sections so there is sufficient material to mirror and supplement the entire Jewish Sabbath cycle. Matthew's Gospel can also be broken into five distinctive blocks of teaching that follow and would have been read during the five great Jewish liturgical festivals.

Goulder and Spong also state that this Christian Gospel / Jewish liturgical Sabbath and Festival lectionary approach is in fact Midrash at work. An example is that of the birth story of Jesus – it is the Midrash of the birth and babyhood of Moses. In this way, Mark, and then Matthew followed by Luke, take the relevant stories from the Jewish Testament and rewrite these into the Jesus context. As such, the Midrash of the synoptic Gospel writers was never intended to be an historically factual record of what Jesus said and did. Doubtless the Gospels were written by taking what Karen Armstrong calls *logos* [factual events remembered by the Apostle Peter, the source for Mark's Gospel] and building the *mythos* [not to be read literally but nonetheless full of Sacred Truth] upon it to explain the on-going Jesus experiences of the writers and their respective communities decades after the execution of Jesus.

STUDY SIX

God Uses the Weak
and Unimportant

Read
Isaiah 7.10–16
Matthew 7.24–27

Sermon
The Season of Advent is celebrated at this time every year, and yet, there is a sense in which we always live in Advent. Traditional Christianity says that we are always waiting for Messiah to come even though it also says that Messiah has come already in Jesus. However, I do not wait for some great cosmic splitting of the skies when Jesus will return from somewhere beyond the blue but I do wait with a sense of anticipation that all of Isaiah's visions considered in our Lectionary readings will come to fruition.

Then, when the earth is filled with the knowledge of God, no one will need to be at war and the Wisdom and Perfect Love found in Jesus will enable him to be seen as the Prince of Peace. But we cannot just wait for these things to pass – we have to be active day by day in working for a world in which the swords of war will be beaten into ploughshares and the spears of war beaten into pruning hooks.

We have to be active day by day in working for a world in which there is equality, justice and peace for all and then, only then, will nation no longer need to take up sword against nation, nor will any nation need to prepare for war. And it is in being active in this work that we ourselves become a daily Advent in our ordinary lives. And it is in that spirit of a daily Advent lived continually by each one of us who are Followers of the Way of Jesus – it is in that Advent spirit that we turn now to consider today's Lectionary reading of Isaiah 7.10–16.

Here Isaiah warns the descendants of David not to put God to the test. Consider again that reading in which the Lord spoke to King Ahaz, the twelfth king of a self-governing Judah, and said directly to him, 'Ask me, your God, for a sign.' But, for some inexplicable reason, King Ahaz got it wrong. He declined the offer and replied, 'I will not ask; I will not put the LORD to the test.' Then First Isaiah takes over the story and attacks the House of David: 'Is it not enough that you try the patience of men? Will you try the patience of my God also?'

Isaiah then said that, in spite of the actions of Ahaz and the House of David in putting God to the test, in the graciousness of God there will be a sign of the coming Immanuel, meaning 'God is with us' – and the sign will be that 'the virgin will be with child and will give birth to a son, and will call him Immanuel'.

I don't want to be a killjoy but we really must remember that Isaiah was not prophesying the birth of Jesus but was referring to the birth of Hezekiah, the son of King Ahaz and Abijah.

But what has all this got to do with you and me? Within all the myths and traditions and stories of the heroes of the Hebrew Testament, Yahweh God was experienced as One who remained gracious and forgiving, continuing to use even the most awful of people. Think again about King Ahaz. He got it wrong. He ignored Isaiah's warning and even sacrificed one of his own sons to a false god. He capitulated too easily to the invading Assyrians with the result that worship of Yahweh was compromised by the introduction of the Assyrian gods. But Yahweh God was still experienced as compassionate and merciful and Ahaz, as the father of Hezekiah, was used in the work of the kingdom.

Think back through some of the leading people of the Hebrew Testament. They were far from perfect. Think of Abraham, the Father of the Nation of Yahweh, and the Father of the Three Religions of the Book: Judaism, Christianity and Islam. But Abraham was a failure who refused to believe the promise of Yahweh God towards him and

Sara, his aged wife. However Yahweh God was still experienced as compassionate and merciful. Still Abraham was used tremendously in the work of the kingdom.

Think of Jacob, the deceiver who wrestled with everybody, including God. Think of Joseph, the childish and conceited youngster who made his brothers so jealous that they pretended that he had been killed by a wild animal when they had, in fact, sold him into slavery into Egypt. Think of Moses, an impulsive leader who was also a murderer. Moses got so many things wrong but Yahweh God was still experienced as compassionate and merciful. Still Jacob and Joseph and Moses were all used tremendously in the work of the kingdom.

And then there was the Judge Gideon, a man who won so many victories for God's people but after defeating the Midianites with just 300 men Gideon accepted the golden earrings taken as spoil in battle. But sadly Gideon got it wrong when he turned the golden earrings into an image of Yahweh and this later became the centre of false worship. There was another Judge, Samson, who was often inebriated and one who had a weakness for women. Think of King David, a man of greatness and of great weakness who abused his power and authority by committing adultery with Bathsheba and then covering his wickedness by murdering the abused husband, the warrior hero Uriah.

Then immediately after David, came his son Solomon, who was in many ways very wise. However his weaknesses were in the very unwise way in which he treated his citizens and in the numerous marriages that he entered into to build political and economic alliances. But Yahweh God was still experienced as compassionate and merciful and all of these were used mightily in the work of the kingdom.

Then resulting from the promise of God in today's reading, came Hezekiah, son of Ahaz, who repaired and re-opened the Temple in Jerusalem. Hezekiah also set about undoing all the evil done by his father. But sadly, Hezekiah listened too often to his political rather than to his religious advisers and made some disastrous decisions as a result. But Yahweh God was still experienced by him as compassionate and merciful and he was used tremendously in the work of the kingdom.

Finally, a very young Jewish girl from a small village in a remote corner of the great Roman Empire found that she was pregnant out of wedlock. But Yahweh God was still experienced as compassionate and merciful and young Mary was used mightily in the work of the kingdom and she gave birth to Jesus of Nazareth.

All this begs the question, 'Why didn't Yahweh God use good and strong people to do the work of the kingdom rather than all these who failed so miserably?' But here is some of the good news of Advent – this collection of inadequates who got it so badly wrong were nevertheless used tremendously in kingdom work. The message is simple and straightforward – even though they were all less than perfect, so we too, who are sometimes inadequate, unwise, and too often lacking in faith and commitment can be used tremendously in the work of the kingdom today!

But, just as Isaiah offered the good news of Immanuel he also issued a warning for his time that is just as applicable to our time. The good news is that we can be used tremendously in kingdom work with all our failings, but the reminder that goes with it is that anyone can be used in kingdom work. The warning in this reminder is that we should not put limits on what the Perfect Unconditional Love that is God can do with the most unlikely of people in the most unlikely of circumstances.

That is part of the surprise of this Advent Season. It is part of daily kingdom work and the strangest of people – even those with whom we would not wish to associate or to call our sisters or brothers – can and often do the work of the kingdom. I can name people I know who would not call themselves either Christian or religious but, by their example, can and often do put me as a Follower of Jesus into the shade when it comes to the kingdom work recorded in the Gospel of Matthew, chapter 25: to stretch out the hand of friendship to the stranger; to give food to the hungry and drink to the thirsty; to clothe the naked and offer shelter to the homeless; to care for the sick and visit the prisoners.

We can be aware of all of this because 'Immanuel' is the truest word within all the Hebrew and Christian Testaments – 'God *is* with us'. And it is in Jesus of Nazareth that we see the Reality of the Advent Hope in all its fulfilment.

It is all kingdom work and it should be all our work. And as we enter this Season of Christmas, let us remember that it is better to give than to receive, and that it is in giving that we receive the real joy of life in all its abundance.

Postscript: Although it is only a word picture, the Truth that underpins Isaiah's vision is real and relevant to today:

> the wolf living with the lamb; the leopard sleeping beside the goat; the calf and the lion being at peace together; the cow feeding with the bear, and their young lying down together; the lion eating straw like the ox; the human baby playing alongside the den of the cobra, and a young child putting his hand into the viper's nest without fear and without harm. And above all this, a little child will lead them (based on Isaiah 11.6–8).

What a hope for the future! But that depends upon us living the kingdom today and every day.

Questions for discussion

1 This study makes the point that, according to the Bible ordinary, inadequate or positively 'bad' people are often used to achieve God's purposes. Can you think of possible modern examples of this?

2 One of this writer's constant themes throughout this series is what the rabbis called *miqra*, the Scriptures as a call to action. He emphasises that 'Faith' is not a matter of intellectual belief but of commitment to a way of life.

There is a much-quoted passage from Albert Schweitzer's *Quest of the Historical Jesus* (1906) doubly significant because his book questioned much of previously held *beliefs* about Jesus:

> We can find no designation which expresses what He is for us. He comes to us as One unknown, without a name, as of old, by the lakeside, He came to those who knew Him not. He speaks to us the same word: 'Follow thou me!' and sets us to the tasks which he has to fulfil for our time. He commands. And to those who obey Him, whether they be wise or simple, He will reveal Himself in the toils, the conflicts, the sufferings which they shall pass through in His fellowship, and, as an ineffable mystery, they shall learn in their own experience Who He is.

After writing that book Schweitzer gave up his distinguished academic and musical careers, retrained as a medical doctor and spent the rest of his life in Equatorial Africa caring for his African patients – admittedly in the paternalistic style of his time – but in obedience to his calling to help repay the debt that he believed the European races owe to the African peoples.

Do you think that Western society thinks of Christians as people who *believe* certain things? Or as people who are committed to a way of life? What do you think defines a Christian?

STUDY SEVEN

ADVENT 4

The Annunciation to Mary

Introductory note

Traditionally the fourth Sunday of Advent focuses on Mary, the mother of Jesus, and in particular the narrative in Luke's Gospel called *The Annunciation*.

The hymns and carols of Christmas are mostly based on the birth narratives in the Gospels of Matthew and Luke – O little town of Bethlehem [*Hymns & Psalms* 113], Away in a manger [94], Silent Night [112], While shepherds watched their flocks by night [120], Hark! The herald angels sing [106], As with gladness men of old did the guiding star behold [212] and so on.

Some people's total knowledge of the First Christmas, as we may call it, is a combination of these carols perhaps re-enforced by a primary school's nativity play. But before even the first 'See him lying on a bed of straw' is sung *critics* are launching forth in their 'too clever by half' challenges: 'There was no star' that did what you say! No census that set out to list all the people in Palestine! And so on. In desperation some of us will have searched the internet for evidence to disprove them or relying perhaps on so-called proof provided by those Christians whose faith depends on the *factual* truth of the birth narratives. And that's where the excitement begins!

To make a narrative of the First Christmas, or a nativity play for that matter, the sequence of events in these two Gospels have been taken and woven together: four parts Luke to one part Matthew and we can't see the joins!

Matthew's Gospel has Joseph and Mary living in Bethlehem, Joseph is the central character, all the instructions come to him in dreams, Mary says nothing. The Wise Men are here, so is Herod with an unhistorical slaying of innocent boys. The Holy Family flees to Egypt and later returns and goes to Nazareth.

Luke's Gospel has Mary as the central character, starting in Nazareth and going to Bethlehem and the rest I think we know for the shepherds and angels, and all the infant events are in Luke.

These are not fairy stories, they are highly structured narratives designed to convince Jews of the claims the first Christians made for Jesus, and among them is the scene that has captured the imagination of artists from before Leonardo da Vinci to the present day. The Annunciation is probably the most popular subject for them.

Read

The Lukan narrative of The Annunciation in Luke 1.26–38.

Sermon

The carols we have both sung and listened to should convince us that truths are conveyed by many means. When we come to the birth narratives the choice is not between believing them as factual truth or not at all but recognising that truth is conveyed by picture language, through metaphor or parable.

Two Biblical scholars, Marcus J. Borg and John Dominic Crossan in *The First Christmas – What the Gospels really teach about Jesus' birth*, have suggested that the birth narratives are like overtures to Matthew and Luke, setting out themes which will appear later in the Gospels.

We associate the word overture with music and in particular with opera. Overtures that offer the most vivid examples of a fore-taste of what is to come are often those written *after* the opera has been written, sometimes even when the conductor is rehearsing the singers and is calling for the overture! It is the judgement of the biblical scholars I have referred to that in this respect the birth narratives are like overtures.

Now we come to the sources and *re*-sources that were used in the compiling of Luke's Gospel.

The intention is *not* to answer questions, least of all whether the events narrated are factually true, but to provide some ways of answering the question, 'what do the birth stories mean?' This is one of my most exciting sermon preparations and I am very grateful for this opportunity to share it with you at this most significant of Christian festivals.

So now to the birth narratives in Luke's Gospel. You will remember what they are: those focusing on Mary and Elizabeth, shepherds and the journeys between Nazareth and Bethlehem and divine messages conveyed by angels. The shadow of the powerful Roman Empire is always there!

Luke's Gospel is likely to have been compiled in Antioch[1], the third largest city in the Roman Empire. It was situated in the bend between the eastern Mediterranean coast and modern Turkey. In the fourth quarter of the first Christian century there was a large and vibrant Christian community there consisting of Jewish Christians both of a very conservative sort, that is those who continued to follow Jewish religious practice, and liberal Jews, those for whom Paul's injunction that in Christ there are neither Jews nor Greeks, accepted Greek believers without the necessity of 'male genital mutilation' as we might call circumcision today!

This Christian community would have had access to Mark's Gospel though certainly not in the form of Pew Bibles! Probably only the Church leaders had a copy. In addition *Sayings of Jesus* had been circulating. Perhaps even in the form of odd jottings or some ambitious collections.[2]

Jewish Christians would have their own Scriptures, particularly the Law[3] and the Prophets. The rest were still being considered as official Jewish Scripture. Significant additional material would have been Jewish religious commentaries of various sorts[4] some of which updated laws and others that were reflections on their Jewish history. Significant figures like Abraham and Sarah are described as childless but with the future of the race depending on their children. Old men and women become parents. Their history is scattered with examples mostly of older people but why not young women too?

No Jew could live under the Roman power system without being affected by the subjection of Judaism and the destruction of their Temple during the Jewish Wars from 70–74 CE, nor without being subjected to demands to worship the Emperor Augustus as divine.

Antony and Cleopatra by courtesy of Hollywood are often the limit of our knowledge of that empire. *I Claudius* might give a better but later picture of imperial power but inscriptions unearthed throughout the former empire, not least in modern Turkey, describe the Emperor Augustus, the vanquisher of Antony and Cleopatra, as Divine, Lord, Redeemer, Liberator and Saviour of the world, even born of a union between a human and a god.

We cannot understand what the titles given to Jesus meant without knowing all that!

You can read most of this on the coin Jesus would have been given in the famous incident, 'Is it right to give taxes to Caesar?' [5]

So the narrative of the Annunciation draws from all these sources, both Jewish and Roman, to write an account that would *ring true* to both Jews and Greeks. Their familiarity with the sources would not distract from the message: God is at work bringing salvation to the world: Jews and Gentiles. Read it, look at the pictures, sing the songs, ancient as well as modern, and it's all there in different ways.

So what is left? Just the great Magnificat which voices the cries of all the marginalised, downtrodden and discriminated against. Imagine yourself a Christian in Antioch who might have used this song before it was incorporated into Luke's Gospel. Would it have spoken to you?

> My soul proclaims the greatness of the Lord,
> my spirit rejoices in God my Saviour,
> who has looked with favour on his lowly servant.
> From this day all generations will call me blessèd:
> the Almighty has done great things for me
> and holy is his name.
> God has mercy on those who fear him,
> from generation to generation.

The Lord has shown strength with his arm
and scattered the proud in their conceit,
casting down the mighty from their thrones
and lifting up the lowly.
God has filled the hungry with good things
and sent the rich away empty.
He has come to the aid of his servant Israel,
to remember the promise of mercy,
the promise made to our forebears,
to Abraham and his children for ever.

Notes
1   Another Antioch is referred to in Acts 13.14, 14.21, 16.6, though this was not
    actually in Pisidia, central modern Turkey.
2   The compiler of Matthew would also have had these. Both Luke and Matthew
    also had sources of other material exclusive to each of them.
3   That is the first five books of the Jewish Scriptures, The Pentateuch. Jewish
    Christians would almost certainly have used the Greek translation of their Scrip-
    tures, from which the Jewish word for 'young women' in Isaiah 7.14 is translated
    with the Greek word for *virgin*.
4   The Talmud and Midrashes.
5   Matthew 22.15–22; Mark 12.13-17; Luke 20.20–26.

The birth stories as parables

This study refers to a book called *The First Christmas* by Marcus Borg
and Dominic Crossan and both this study and the next are based on
their scholarship. The book itself is clear and concise but packed
with illuminating contextual references and biblical parallels.

The study adopts Borg's and Crossan's description of the birth
stories as a parabolic overture to the main themes of each Gospel.
The question these authors set out to answer is not, 'Did these things
really happen?' but 'What is the *meaning* of these stories?' The truth
of these stories as they present them is their truth as parables, leav-
ing aside the question of their truth or otherwise as biographical
fact. The purpose of these studies is to enable the members of the
group to explore some of this meaning for themselves.

Questions for discussion

1 Read Luke 1.5–24, Genesis 17 and Genesis 18.1–19.
   What similarities do you notice between the story of John
   the Baptist's birth and Isaac's?
   What other Old Testament stories come to mind?

2 Read 1 Samuel 2.1–10.
   Does Hannah's song remind you of anything?

3 Read the following note on the virgin birth.
   Do you see a possible significance in the parallels with
   Roman claims for the Emperor Augustus?

Note on the virgin birth

Virginal conception not virgin birth
We need first to clarify what we mean when we talk about the
'virgin birth'.

The Gospels speak about Jesus being *virginally conceived not
virginally born.*

The perpetual virginity of Mary was a doctrine later developed in
the Roman Catholic Church as was the 'immaculate conception' of
Mary, meaning that Mary herself was conceived without the stain
of original sin (a doctrine developed during the middle ages but
declared an official doctrine by the Vatican in 1854) and the
Assumption to heaven of the Virgin Mary (without going through
death) a doctrine which developed during the fifth century and was
declared an article of faith by Pius XII in 1950. Some of these doctrines have been subject to re-appraisal since the Second Vatican
Council in the 1960s.

Text from Isaiah 7.14
'A virgin / young woman shall conceive and bear a son,' quoted in
Matthew 1.23.

The Hebrew version of the Old Testament text reads 'a young

woman'. The Greek version, the version most widely used in New Testament times reads 'a virgin'. Matthew uses Midrash to link Mary's virginity with the Old Testament text. Later Gentile Christians took it as a 'prophecy'.

Divine/human conception

It was common in the Greco/Roman world to consider that outstanding leaders were the product of a union between a god and a human being. At the time of Jesus' birth it was the Emperor Augustus who was pronounced divine as the result of a union between his human mother, Atia and the god, Apollo, although he also claimed divinity through his adoption by Julius Caesar who was himself called a Son of God and claimed descent from Venus. His status as divine was propagated throughout the Empire and, in a time of mass illiteracy, was 'advertised' by means of ubiquitous statuary (whose remains have been studied by archaeologists) and on their coins.

His titles were Divine, Son of God, God from God, Lord, Redeemer, Liberator and Saviour of the world. The Roman Empire itself was claimed to be the fifth and final universal kingdom that would bring peace to the nations.

To claim these titles for Jesus was in itself an act of subversion.

Pax Romana was peace through submission to Roman victory.

The peace of the Christian gospel was peace through justice to the poor. (Re-read Mary's song, The Magnificat.)

While divine conception with the pagan gods involved physical intimacy, the Gospels assert Mary's virginity and do not imply a physical union with the 'High God' of the Jews. This is asserted even at the risk of exposing Mary to the charge of adultery and Jesus to the charge of bastardy, a charge to which Matthew's account of Joseph's doubts leaves them open and a charge made by later critics of Christianity.

STUDY EIGHT

A BIBLE STUDY

The Christmas Stories

In Study Seven the preacher took the birth stories from Matthew's and Luke's Gospels and showed how we usually wove them together to make up a nativity play. His focus was then on Luke's Gospel and the meaning of the story of the Annunciation to Mary and many of the most familiar Christmas stories that appear only in Luke. It was not possible in the confines of a sermon and an act of worship to explore all of the discoveries that had caused him to find this 'one of his most exciting sermon preparations'. The following Bible study is intended to offer the readers the chance to go through the same process of discovery for themselves.

Athough Matthew and Luke used some common sources, they did write two separate accounts with different audiences in mind. Let us see what emerges if we read them separately. So many extra legends have developed around these stories the aim is to see what is actually there in the New Testament and to try to understand why Matthew and Luke wrote these stories when Mark had simply plunged straight in with the story of Jesus as an adult, going to John for baptism.

Matthew's account written with Jewish Christians in mind
Read Matthew, Chapters 1 and 2 as though you have never read it before, at least noting (if you find it too boring to read!) Chapter 1, verses 1–17. What does his story consist of?

17 verses of genealogy
• Boring to us but clearly of significance to the readership Matthew had in mind.

8 verses about Joseph
- About Joseph's dilemma when he discovers that the woman to whom he is betrothed is already pregnant. He plans to divorce her 'privately' rather than obey the strict requirements of the Law (Deuteronomy 22.20–21) and subject her to stoning.
- About Joseph's first dream. An angel appears and tells him that the baby is a holy child conceived by the Holy Spirit and is to be called 'Emmanuel' (God with us) as in Isaiah 7.14.
- About Joseph's marriage to Mary – not consummated until after the birth of Jesus. He names the baby Jesus (Saviour).

12 verses about the Wise Men and the 'wicked king', Herod
- Introducing the Wise Men from the East.
- Introducing the 'wicked king' Herod and his plot. He is told that it is prophesised (Micah 5.2) that the baby will be born in Bethlehem (the city of the shepherd king, David) so asks the Wise Men to tell him when and where they find the baby.
- Telling of the visit of the Wise Men to Mary and the baby. They offer their three gifts.
- About the Wise Men's dream. They return the other way.

3 verses about Joseph's second dream and the escape to Egypt
- About Joseph's second dream warning him about the 'wicked king'.
- About the escape to Egypt. Midrash – 'Out of Egypt I called my Son' (Hosea 11.1).

2 verses about the massacre of the infants by the 'wicked king'
- Lamentation (Jeremiah 31.15).

6 verses about Joseph's third and fourth dreams
- Joseph has a third dream and returns to Israel.
- Joseph has a fourth dream and makes their home in Nazareth. The play on the word 'Nazarene' (a dedicated person) makes a parallel with the stories of Samson, Samuel and John the Baptist (1 Samuel 22; Judges 13.4–5; Luke 8.15).

Total
17 verses of genealogy
17 verses about Joseph
14 verses about the wise men and the wicked king

Dreams play a large part in the story. Joseph has four dreams. The wise men have one dream.

There is nothing about the actual birth of Jesus – only a reference in Matthew 1.25 and 2.11 that he has already been born.

Questions for discussion

1 Who is the main character in Matthew's story?

2 What other major character in the Old Testament had dreams?

3 How many wise men are there and how many kings?

4 Where are Mary and Joseph at the beginning of the story?

5 Where was Jesus born – at home or in a stable? (Matthew 2.11)

6 What other major character in Jewish history spends his infancy in Egypt?

7 What other 'wicked king' in Jewish history plans the massacre of Jewish boy babies?

8 Do you detect 'Midrash' at work here or is it all a fulfilment of prophecy?

We shall look at both genealogies in Study Nine.

Luke's account written with Gentiles in mind
Now read Luke 1.5 to 2.52.

20 verses about Zechariah and Elizabeth
- Introducing Zechariah and Elizabeth, an old and barren couple.
- About Zechariah's vision of the angel Gabriel while serving as a priest in the Temple in Jerusalem. The baby is to be like Elijah but is to be called John.
- He is rebuked for his doubts and struck dumb.
- Elizabeth becomes pregnant. Remains secluded for five months.

12 verses about the visit of Gabriel to Mary in Nazareth
- The annunciation to Mary. We are told that Mary is a virgin betrothed to Joseph. Gabriel tells her that she will have a holy baby and she is to call him Jesus.
- He will be called Son of the Most High. He will have the throne of his ancestor, David. He will reign over the 'house of Jacob'. His kingdom will be everlasting.
- He will be called Son of God.
- Mary is told that Elizabeth is six months pregnant.
- Mary accepts her calling.

16 verses about Mary's visit to Elizabeth in Judea and Mary's song
- Mary visits Elizabeth in the hill country of Judea. Elizabeth's baby leaps in greeting.
- Mary's song.
- Mary stays with Elizabeth for three months. (By their reckoning in lunar months she goes home a month before Elizabeth's baby is due.)

24 verses about the birth and naming of John the Baptist
- Elizabeth has her baby and her neighbours and relatives rejoice with her.
- The baby is circumcised at eight days.
- Elizabeth says that the baby is to be called John. Others think he should be called Zechariah.

- Zechariah writes on the tablet that he is to be called John. General amazement. His speech is restored.
- Zechariah's song – the Benedictus. He celebrates God's promise of redemption for Israel.
- John grows up and goes into the wilderness.

19 verses about the birth of Jesus in Bethlehem and the visit of the shepherds
- The Emperor Augustus decrees a census. Joseph takes Mary from Nazareth in Galilee to Bethlehem in Judea (the city of David).
- The birth of Jesus. He is cradled in a manger because there was no room for them in the inn.
- The angels appear to the shepherds, announce the birth of the Messiah and Saviour in the city of David and sing the Angels' Song promising peace on earth. They visit Mary and Joseph and the baby. Mary 'treasured these words in her heart'.

28 verses about Jesus being taken to the Temple but growing up in Nazareth
- 3 verses Jesus is circumcised and named Jesus.
- Jesus is taken to the Temple for purification and dedication. His parents offer the prescribed sacrifices.
- Simeon, a righteous man looking for 'the consolation of Israel' Simeon takes the baby in his arms and sings the Benedictus. The salvation brought by Jesus will be a light to lighten the Gentiles and will bring glory to Israel. He blesses the parents but warns Mary that a sword will pierce her soul.
- Anna, an 84-year-old widow, speaks about the child to all who were looking for the redemption of Israel.
- The childhood of Jesus in Nazareth.
- The 12-year-old Jesus goes with his parents to Passover in Jerusalem as was their annual family custom.
- Jesus stays behind with the teachers in the Temple and rebukes his parents for not understanding but obediently returns to Naz - areth with them. Mary again 'treasures these things in her heart'.
- Jesus grows up.

Total

44 verses about Zechariah, Elizabeth and John

47 verses about Mary and the birth of Jesus and her visit to Elizabeth

28 verses about Jesus' circumcision, purification and visit to the Temple for the Passover.

Questions for discussion

1 Who is the main character in Luke's story?

2 Who is the focus of the parallel story? Why do you think this is?

3 Where (geographically) does the story begin and end?

4 Why do you think there is no massacre of the children and no escape to Egypt?

5 Luke's account is full of songs. How many? It is generally believed that the songs were early Christian hymns and pre-date the writing of the Gospel.

6 Look carefully at the songs and summarise the messages they give. Do you think they were subversive?

STUDY NINE

EPIPHANY

The Wise Men

Read
Matthew 2.1–18

Sermon
Most people have heard of *or* can even sing 'We three kings …' yet where do we get the number *three* from? And how do we know they *were* kings? It says 'Wise Men', Magi, number unspecified. Astrologers perhaps, but how were *they* to know that an unusual celestial occurrence was of any significance, and if so what?

Now this *already* sounds like a debunking of the Christmas story, one so familiar to us from countless Nativity plays, but that's not *my* intention.

A simple overview of the birth narratives would show us that the accounts in the Gospels of Matthew and Luke are incompatible. They *cannot* be woven together into story as so many of our Nativity plays do.

The choice in front of us is not simply are they *fact* or *fable* but could they perhaps be *parables*, that is narratives with a meaning. I'll not say 'stories' again because that word comes loaded with the wrong connotation. In my childhood being told not to tell *stories* meant 'don't tell lies'! Parables are a form of speech just like poetry; it is a way of using language.

We don't ask whether there was a *real* Samaritan who rode from Jerusalem to Jericho and came across a man who had been mugged. We might, however, say he was stupid stopping like he did on a road notorious for ambushes!

When we lived in Rome an American Baptist minister we knew

did just that on the road to Rome from the coastal airport at
Fiumicino. He stopped his car and went to help a man at the road-
side who appeared to be injured and was himself mugged and
stripped and left naked.

The story of the Good Samaritan is among the best-known
parables of Jesus along with that of the Prodigal Son, the Workers
in the Vineyard and so on.

In each narrative something happens. Often the meaning lies in
just one pithy saying, 'a bolt from the blue' one New Testament
scholar called it, though frequently preachers do unpack them.
Dr William Sangster, the famous minister at the Central Hall, West-
minster, did just that with 'Old Mother Hubbard' in his book on
The Art of Preaching – as an example of what *not* to do! 'She was *old*,
not young, not even middle aged, she was *old*, she went to the
cupboard, she didn't run or skip, too old for that, she just went',
and so on ...

However this can be done *properly* with the longer parables.
Could this not be done with the birth stories? Doesn't this provide
another way of looking at them other than fact or fable? Either
torturing ourselves to make them true in a factual sense – I've been
waiting for the annual claim to have identified the Star of the East
– or rubbishing them as fable and producing yet one more book
claiming to have undermined the whole Christian faith?

Mark's Gospel, the earliest one, contains no such birth narrative.
John provides quite a different form of opening to the life and
works of Jesus which parallels the first chapter of Genesis.
In the case of both Matthew and Luke the life and works of Jesus,
are placed between bookends, as it were, each providing extended
parables of the 'before' and 'after'.

We are invited to explore these extended parables, to consider
how they were constructed and what they are saying to us in *our*
day and age.

As we have seen before ...

Two New Testament scholars, Marcus Borg and John Dominic
Crossan, writing together in this book, *The First Christmas* suggest

the idea of an 'overture', a narrative written *after* the main body of the Gospels of Matthew and Luke had been compiled, which encapsulate the themes which occur within those Gospels.

We come across overtures when we listen to operas; to some *that* tedious bit of instrumental music before the curtain goes up and the action starts and the actor/singers start telling the real *story*.

Opera was something we were introduced to in Italy by a friend ready to extend our life-experiences to include what we came to discover is a wonderful source entertainment and more.

Living in Italy at the time with its great opera houses in Milan, Rome and Naples and every town with its smaller venue I started to read up about them. What surprised me was that composers like Verdi and Puccini left the overtures to last and were still writing them while the singers were learning their lines and practising the arias etc. and the impresarios tearing their hair out waiting for it. Innocently I assumed that the overture was written first. How wrong could I be?

Then as my knowledge of different operas increased and I became more familiar with the music I recognised parts of tunes from the body of the opera appearing in the overture. At first I thought of this as a quick way of getting an overture produced by the composer for the orchestra to play, later the dawning came that in the overture we are *introduced* to what we are about to hear and see. This is our *index* to the story.

And so it could be with the birth narratives to the Gospels of Matthew and Luke.

The writers of this book *The First Christmas* propose that the Christmas narratives [I nearly said 'stories' again!] are primarily *parabolic overtures* but based on biblical tradition rather than on historic fact, a Gospel in miniature.

So when the birth narratives of Matthew and Luke are combined into a single Christmas story as in our traditional Christmas Nativity play we do have the Gospel in miniature; a Gospel that is missed *entirely* if one insists that the narratives are factual accounts of actual events. That *really* is not seeing the wood for the trees!

One of the major aspects of the ministry of Jesus that is *clear* in Luke but also there in Matthew is the universal nature of the Gospel. Matthew ends with the Great Commission to go out into all the world and preach the gospel to all ... (Matthew 28.19–20).

This is an aspect of Judaism that was there in their Scriptures (for example, our first lesson) but gradually got pushed out through periods of persecution and suffering. At that time they were anxious to preserve the purity of both religion *and* race.

How does this apply to the narrative of the Wise Men?

This begins with being drawn by a great light, then the journey, visiting King Herod for information, the searching of the Jewish Scriptures by learned men for an answer for Herod, their arrival at the house in Bethlehem where we are to assume Joseph and Mary already lived and *not* as pilgrims in a stable as in Luke, being warned in a dream not to return to Herod but to go another way, Herod's anger when he realised he had been duped and then his murderous enterprise, meanwhile the Holy Family went to Egypt (another dream for Joseph), their return but not to their home in Judea but north to Galilee and Nazareth ... now we have Jesus at the same place Luke has him, and ready for his ministry.

To examine each part in detail and compare it with obvious parallels with Moses and the Exodus would take weeks, we haven't got that – so let's look at the whole picture and see how it links expressly to Epiphany, the Manifestation of Christ to the Gentiles, that's today commemoration.

Right there at the *beginning* a group of people representing the non-Jews come into the picture. Jews referred to all others as 'the nations' from which we get the word 'Gentiles'. Originally it didn't seem to have the derogatory meaning we have become accustomed to.

In spite of years of being ostracised by the Jews, the Gentiles enter the birth narrative at the very *beginning* – and that is a very good place to start! The Jewish expectation was that *their* religion would be so luminous that it would attract the 'nations' to Jerusalem.

The conclusion of Matthew's Gospel is that *that* is not enough; believers must go out into all the world, that is to all the nations.

That's why the wise men are there in the birth narrative.

That's why Jesus' kingdom is not of this world like Herod's fascist dictatorship.

Are we like the Wise Men who follow the light and refuse to comply with the ruler's plot to destroy it? Or are we like Herod, filled with fear and willing to use whatever means necessary to maintain power, even violence and slaughter?

The Wise Men certainly changed *their* plans as a result of *their* journey, as the Prodigal Son was to change his life as the result of his journey.

The Genealogies
Luke 3.23–28
Matthew 1.1–17
Luke introduces his version of Jesus' genealogy after the baptism by John. Why do you think this might be?

Matthew considers the genealogy so important that he places it right at the beginning of his Gospel.

Have you ever looked at them before? Are you curious to understand why they take up so many verses in the Gospels?

If you enjoy detective stories read the chapter on the genealogies in Borg and Crossan's book. He summarises the differences as follows:

- Matthew counts forward through the generations from **Abraham to Jesus.**
- Luke count backwards through the generations from **Jesus to Adam, the son of God.**
- Matthew is interested in counting 14 generations from Abraham to David, 14 generations from David to the Exile, 14 generations from the Exile to the Messiah.
- He is not strictly accurate in his mathematics but his intention is to demonstrate the significance of the expectation of the Messiah.

- Luke and Matthew have several different names in their genealogies, including different names for Joseph's father.
- They both avoid making the implication that Joseph was the biological father of Jesus, Luke by his note in parenthesis and Matthew by referring to Joseph as the husband of Mary but, by his use of a feminine word for 'of whom' calls Jesus Mary's son but not Joseph's.
- Following the custom of their patriarchal society they both name fathers rather than mothers in the genealogies but Matthew names four special women from the Old Testament.
- In Luke, Jesus is a new Adam and a new Son of God and his baptism by water and the Spirit links back to Genesis 1.1–2. Jesus begins his ministry after his baptism and this begins a new Creation.

Borg and Crossan also draw a parallel with the genealogical claims of the Emperor Augustus, who traced his ancestry back to Venus the child of Jupiter, the Roman high god. Both Matthew and Luke are making a political and theological statement by composing these genealogies, not establishing biological facts.

Questions for discussion

1 Why do you think Matthew traces Jesus ancestry back to Abraham? – and Luke traces it back to Adam?

2 Had you previously noticed that in Matthew's account Jesus is born, not in the stable of an inn but in a house (Matthew 2.11), the family's home, as they were already living in Bethlehem and did not move to Nazareth until they returned from Egypt? Why do you think that Luke's account has become so popular that Matthew's version has been wiped from our minds? Do you think that there is any link between this fact and the message in Mary's song?

3   Do you see a connection between the presence of the Wise Men in Matthew's version and the Song of Simeon in Luke's?

4   What connection can you see between the Christmas stories and the political situation in Israel at the time?

5   What additional legends have been added to the birth stories in the traditions of the Church through the centuries? What are the names of the Wise Men?

6   Do we know anything else about them?

7   What is the significance of the three gifts?

8   What titles has Mary been given by Roman Catholics? What pictures and statues of her can you think of? Beside Christ at the Last Judgement (Sistine Chapel). Holding the body of her son after the Crucifixion. Wearing a halo. Wearing a crown. The black Madonna. Henry Moore's statues of the Madonna.

9   Why do you think that Christmas worship includes so much music and singing?

10 Why do you think these stories have made such a strong appeal to the Christian imagination? Let your own imagination play around the stories – perhaps compose your own carol or nativity play.

11 By understanding more about the original purpose of the Christmas stories will you be able to appreciate them in a more adult way while still enjoying them with a childlike imagination? How should we answer children when they ask, 'Did it really happen like that?'?

STUDY TEN

SO YOU THINK IT'S ALL OVER?

The Baby Grows Up!

Read
Luke 2.41–52

Sermon
With this reading we come to the end of the birth narrative in Luke's Gospel and a strange one it is as you can see!

Next week the Lectionary jumps right into the ministry of John the Baptist, though some of the passages from Luke's Gospel about the Baptist have already been read during Advent. From now onwards the third Gospel is written in a very different style from that of the birth narratives.

We are used to seeing the Magi or the Wise Men together with the Holy Family and the shepherds in our Christmas Nativities displays, but the Magi have been taken from Matthew's Gospel and woven into that of Luke's narrative to make a seamless garment.

The birth narrative in Matthew is written from the point of view of Joseph; if you followed it through in Studies Seven and Eight you will have seen this. Like another Joseph of the distant past in Jewish history, the place and significance of dreams is paramount, and the parallels appear intentional. And they don't end there!

Luke, on the other hand, relates the stories from the point of view of Mary, concluding with the sentence that she 'treasured all these things in her heart'.

It has been pointed out that Luke's Gospel begins and ends in the Temple in Jerusalem.

It opens with Zechariah's vision in the Temple – he was father of John the Baptist (1.8) – and ends with the post-Resurrection scene of the disciples who returned to Jerusalem with great joy, where they were continually in the Temple praising God (24.53).

But this *doesn't* take account of today's reading which in a way concludes the birth narrative *twelve years on* and in the Temple too.

Or is this passage really the start of the next part of the Gospel?

In some ways it continues the style of the birth narrative without being really part of them.

There is a hymn by Fred Pratt Green which has the lines:

> So when the dove descended
> On him, the Son of Man,
> The hidden years had ended,
> The age of grace began.
>
> (*Hymns & Psalms* 132 verse 2)

Does the phrase *'the hidden years'* mean anything to you? The title of a book you read as a child? Or was it read to you?

What does it mean? It refers to the years of Jesus' life from childhood to the start of his ministry. The New Testament says nothing about these years except the part we read today.

During the early years of the Jewish-Christian communities when there was still a strong desire to persuade their fellow non-believing Jews that Jesus *was* Messiah, *their* Messiah, the challenge to Judaism was set in the context of Jesus as a loyal and devoted Jew. Certainly Jesus is shown in Luke's Gospel challenging the contemporary Jewish attitude of the Law, the Torah, but it was as one born and brought up *within* its traditions. Today's Bible reading underlines that. His was a traditional Jewish family, doing the things expected of them, including the annual visits to Jerusalem, and fulfilling the customs expected of them. Perhaps this visit was for Jesus' bar mitzvah. The message of this passage is: *'This* is the basis on which you must understand the life and ministry of Jesus'.

The picture of the child Jesus amazing his adult religious listeners in the Jerusalem Temple with his perception, with his astute questions and knowledgeable answers fits in well with the 'hidden year' portrayal of Jesus in the non-canonical writings but one that was obviously acceptable to the hearers and readers of the Third Gospel. 'If Jesus could be like this as a child, don't be surprised at his adult life and work,' it seems to be saying.

Jewish hearers could accept this explanation without the need to ask whether the events were *literally* true. It *was true* because it rang true within the style of religious teaching with which they were familiar, that is it answered the question 'What does it *mean*?'

Towards the end of the first century when the first three Gospels began to be copied and made into cumbersome parchments books, not scrolls as we see shown in Jewish synagogues, the majority of Christians were by now Greek-speaking Gentiles unfamiliar with the religious teaching traditions of the Jews and living in a world of lords many and gods many. To them the birth narratives in Matthew and Luke were, it seems, taken at their face value, and so the tradition of the literal interpretation of the Bible began that in these days is the cause of so much controversy and acrimony in the Church.

But 25 to 45 years before *that* the Apostle Paul had been travelling across the Eastern Mediterranean lands of the Roman Empire, founding local churches and writing letters to them. It is in these Letters that we find the earliest written references to Jesus but the apostle had almost nothing to say about the birth, life and ministry of Jesus *before* the Crucifixion. His focus is almost entirely on Jesus' passion, death, Resurrection and exaltation. These are the subjects that concerned Paul and about which preached and wrote.

There is one passage above all others much-loved by Methodists, it is the one which Charles Wesley takes and amplifies in the line he 'emptied himself of ...?' Of what? '... all but love'. The scriptural passage doesn't have '... of all but love' but Charles Wesley knew a truth when he included it!

The hymn? 'And can it be that I should gain an interest in the Saviour's love' (*Hymns & Psalms* 216 verse 3). And the passage is from Paul's Letter to ... ? The Philippians. Chapter 2, verses 5–11, but it begins:

If then there is any encouragement in Christ, any consolation

from love, any sharing in the Spirit, any compassion and sym-
pathy, make my joy complete: be of the same mind, having the
same love, being in full accord and of one mind. Do nothing
from selfish ambition or conceit, but in humility regard others as
better than yourselves. Let each of you look not to your own
interests, but to the interests of others. Let the same mind be in
you that was in Christ Jesus,

> who, though he was in the form of God,
>> did not regard equality with God
>> as something to be exploited,
> but emptied himself,
>> taking the form of a slave,
>> being born in human likeness.
> And being found in human form,
>> he humbled himself
>> and became obedient to the point of death –
>> even death on a cross.

> Therefore God also highly exalted him
>> and gave him the name
>> that is above every name,
> so that at the name of Jesus
>> every knee should bend,
>> in heaven and on earth and under the earth,
> and every tongue should confess
>> that Jesus Christ is Lord,
>> to the glory of God the Father.

In recent years this passage has usually been printed in verse form.
    It is thought by many New Testament scholars that this was an
early Christian hymn, known to Paul and incorporated by him in
this passage which is *actually* an appeal to the Philippian Christians
to live in harmony: be humble and self-giving as Jesus was!
    Some scholars, notably Borg and Crossan in their recent book,
The First Paul, believe it was written by Paul himself but anyway it

is perhaps 'the fullest concise distillation of the theology of the radical Paul'.

Geza Vermes, a Jewish scholar with a Christian background, claims this passage reflects a later date, probably the early second century CE.

Either way, this passage has been built into the faith of many Christians.

For Paul Jesus had been born, obviously, but only two passages say anything about the significance of his birth. The first passage of note is Galatians 4.4–5:

> But when the fullness of time had come, God sent his Son, born of a woman, born under the law, in order to redeem those who were under the law, so that we might receive adoption as children.

No details of Jesus' birth. It seems that these did *not* interest Paul.

In Paul's Letter to the Christians in Rome he starts with:

> ... the gospel concerning his Son, who was descended from David according to the flesh and was declared to be Son of God with power according to the spirit of holiness by resurrection from the dead, Jesus Christ our Lord (Romans 1.4–5).

... and those two passages are all we can glean from the earliest New Testament writings about the birth of Jesus.

Paul's faith, as we read it in his letters, as he explains it to his young churches, was about Jesus' passion, suffering, death and exaltation. He manages, so it seems, without Christmas.

Do you remember the Live Aid song written to accompany aid to the starving millions in sub-Saharan Africa some year ago: 'Do they know it's Christmas?'? 'So what,' Paul might have said! He and fellow Christians until the second and perhaps third century managed without it too!

Who else can't do without Christmas? Retailers? Travel Agents? Tabloid newspapers who love to be self-righteous when they think the traditional Christmas is being threatened! Militant atheists too who look forward to their annual attack on the dating of

Christmas coinciding with the ancient winter festival of Saturnalia.
A local Advent and Christmas Services leaflet had for 31 December:

> Have we got anything left over from Christmas?
> Bring along an already-discarded present: toy, book, garment or
> even a puppy or hamster.
> What have we left to take into the New Year?

I haven't noticed anything ... have you brought anything?

So what is it that we *take* into the New Year from our Christmas
celebrations this year that can make a significant difference to us?

Did we go to Bethlehem to see a King as the Wise Men did?

Did we hear the angels sing?

What do we bring from the birth stories that will change our
lives?

Birth narratives in the third Gospel, New Testament scholars now
believe, were included to challenge the Jews to accept Jesus' radical
re-assessment of them. If this Jesus was to be accepted by the Jewish contemporaries of the first Jewish Christians, then *they* needed
to be re-assured that this Jesus was a thoroughly loyal Jew and one
grounded in their scriptures.

So the Christian-Jewish teacher used an acceptable Jewish
method to establish Jesus as a King in the Davidic line, shown as
The Coming One by the prophets, belonging to a devoted Jewish
family and so on.

What of ourselves? Do we have grounds for hope that Christmas
means anything to us?

Yes, I am sure we do.

If anyone seeks to relate the Jesus of the Gospels to this present
age and attempts to make faith and the Church relevant to a very
different world from the one in which the non-Jewish, Gentile
Christians took the Jewish birth narratives and *literalised* them,
then we too must be well-grounded in the Bible and in an understanding of it. This means treating the Bible seriously, seeking to
understand what was being said at a particular time, what it was
intended to convey, and how it was to be lived out.

So today, the last day of the year, if you want a New Year Resolution take this one: I will treat the Bible seriously, seeking to understand what was being said at a particular time, what it was intended to convey, and how it was to be lived out, and how we should live it out today.

And empty ourselves of all but love ... that's our job too!

Explanatory note on the hidden years

In the first few centuries after the time numerous legends developed about the childhood of Jesus and his miraculous powers during his infancy. A major collection of such stories was *The Infancy Gospel of Thomas* of which the earliest surviving written fragments date from the fifth century CE and some other fragments that date from the fifteenth century CE. The original probably dates from the second century. Most of the stories show the infant Jesus as what modern eyes would see as a rather revolting, precocious child, using his miraculous powers to get his own way and to take his revenge on any who crossed him, rather like Roald Dahl's mischievous character, Matilda, who uses magic to thwart the adults she dislikes, but with greater malice and power than her.

One of the more attractive stories is the tale of how he was found by Joseph at the age of five, modelling twelve clay sparrows on a Sabbath day. When Joseph rebuked him, he clapped his hands and the sparrows came to life and flew away, chirping. This is one of the Jesus stories that is repeated in the Q'ran which dates from the sixth century CE.

Having taken from Luke's Gospel the story of how at the age of twelve he stayed behind in the Temple to continue his discussion with his teachers the author has added earlier tales of arrogant superiority towards those who tried to teach him the Greek and Hebrew alphabets.

Explanatory note on *The Gospel of Thomas*

The Infancy Gospel of Thomas should not be confused with the *Gospel of Thomas* fragments which were first discovered at an

Egyptian site called Oxyrhyncus between 1896 and 1907 and more pages of which were discovered with 51 other ancient documents in 1945 near another Egyptian town called Nag Hammadi. *The Gospel of Thomas* consists of 114 verses (called 'Logions') of Jesus' teaching, much of it familiar from the New Testament Gospels, but without information about the events of his life. It is generally considered by scholars as composed about the same time or even earlier than those Gospels.

Questions for discussion

1 Elaine Pagels, in her book *The Gnostic Gospels,* suggests that one of the main differences between the early Christian communities who were given the name 'Gnostic' and those who were obedient to the bishops and what they defined as orthodox was that the Gnostics thought of themselves as on a spiritual journey and seekers of the truth while those who were orthodox thought they had found it. In order to discover the relevance of the gospel story for our post-Enlightenment, post-modern age the writers of this book have been 'seekers' on a continuing journey of faith. Have you found it helpful to seek truth in this way or have you found it disturbing?

2 People in the first century were impressed by miracle and would have admired the powers of the child Jesus as presented in *The Infancy Gospel of Thomas* while we in this post-Enlightenment scientific age can find miracle embarrassing. Early liberal theologians tended to look for naturalistic explanations of miracles in the Gospels, that were rarely convincing and were often seen as a 'watering down' of the Bible.

More recent theologians like Borg and Crossan have helped us to see that these stories were never intended to be accurate factual accounts of actual happenings but were interpretations of the Jesus story within the context of the Jewish faith. The question they are answering is not 'Did these events actually happen that way?' but 'Why did Jesus perform these particular miracles and what was their meaning within their context?

Several of our studies have interpreted the Gospel stories in the Jewish context in this way. Have you found this approach helpful?